What Jesus Really Meant

What Jesus Really Meant

Richard L. Litke

Pacific Press® Publishing Association
Nampa, Idaho
Oshawa, Ontario, Canada
www.pacificpress.com

Cover design by Steve Lanto
Inside design by Aaron Troia

The author assumes full responsibility for the accuracy of all facts and quotations as cited in this book. Many of the definitions used in the callouts are taken from Walter Bauer, William F. Arndt, and F. Wilbur Gingrich, *A Greek-English Lexicon of the New Testament and Other Early Christian Literature* (Chicago: The University of Chicago Press, 1957).

You can obtain additional copies of this book by calling toll-free 1-800-765-6955 or by visiting http://www.adventistbookcenter.com.

Library of Congress Cataloging-in-Publication Data:
Litke, Richard L.
What Jesus really meant : challenging passages in the New Testament /
Richard L. Litke.
     p. cm.
ISBN 13: 978-0-8163-2479-8 (pbk.)
ISBN 10: 0-8163-2479-4 (pbk.)
1. Bible. N.T.—Criticism, interpretation, etc. 2. Bible. N.T.—
Language, style. 3. Jesus Christ—Teachings. I. Title.
BS2361.3.L57 2011
225.6'6—dc22
                                                            2011003642

11 12 13 14 15 • 5 4 3 2 1

Table of Contents

Preface

The Bible's New Testament seems to have been written clearly enough for everyone to understand. Not only are the narratives in the four Gospels, for instance, attractive and compelling, but they also treat the life of Christ in such a very basic way that they seem almost devoid of any bothersome complexities. In fact, people often say that even a child can understand them.

However, even these simple stories contain expressions here and there—sometimes almost tucked out of sight—that beg for expansion and explanation. Likewise, the various epistles of the New Testament contain a few words and phrases that are not particularly easy for the casual reader to understand.

For example, why did Jesus call the Syro-Phoenician woman a "dog"? (Mark 7:24–30). What did Jesus mean when He said we're to love our enemies? (Matthew 5:44). How can He expect us to love them while they're mistreating us? And doesn't what the apostle Paul wrote in Philippians 1:23 teach that as soon as Christians die, they go to be with the Lord?

Questions of this sort—and many more like them—demand clear, fitting answers so we can feel certain that we're understanding God's Word and His will for us correctly. These are the kinds of questions I answer in the pages that follow. I hope these short explanatory chapters will increase the understanding of and appreciation for the Scriptures of those who love the Lord and who honor His Word.

As far as reputable scholars can determine, the individual books of the New Testament were originally composed in the *Koinē* dialect of the Greek language. This means that many of our explanations of difficult passages must give due consideration to the Greek word or words that the original author used, so in the explanations that follow, you can expect to see references to Greek words. However, when I use those Greek words, I'll provide clear translations to make them understandable. I intend this book to make the Bible an easier "tool" for busy pastors and educated lay people to use—a goal it certainly won't reach if it were just another book of cumbersome and difficult explanations.

In presenting this volume to you, the reader, I would also like to express my heartfelt thanks to Mrs. Jackie Larson—now, Mrs. Jackie Larson Litke!—who helped prepare it for its publication by graciously keying the manuscript into a computer. And I want to add a note of appreciation to Mrs. Cathy Salzman, who made a number of valuable suggestions and corrections that have enhanced the content.

This volume comes accompanied by my heartfelt prayer that it may make a highly useful contribution to those who love their Lord and who earnestly hunger to understand His Word more perfectly.

CHAPTER 1

The Language Jesus Spoke

The question posed in the title of this chapter is an important one because the language Christ spoke affects how we should understand certain passages in the New Testament. Some New Testament statements, in fact, have meaning only if we know the language of the person who spoke or wrote them. So, it may be helpful at the very beginning of this book to consider briefly the language used by those who spoke and wrote in the New Testament period.

Let's begin by noting what is probably obvious to most readers of the Bible—that the various personalities of the New Testament were, with only a few exceptions, members of the Hebrew race. We might assume, then, that every one of them must have spoken and written in the Hebrew language. However, this assumption is wrong. We now know that in Christ's time, Hebrew wasn't anyone's common, day-to-day language.

What language, then, did the New Testament writers use? And why weren't they speaking and writing in Hebrew?

Many biblical scholars today believe that, originally, Abraham's native tongue was the ancient Mesopotamian language called Sumerian. Ur, Abraham's hometown, was located in the lower Mesopotamian Valley, and the people who lived there spoke Sumerian. Then, when Abraham and his family migrated from Mesopotamia to the southern part of Palestine, they adopted the language of the Canaanites, who were their neighbors. So Abraham's descendants, the Hebrews, spoke a dialect of the ancient Canaanite language. Consequently, when we speak of the "Hebrew" language or read in some commentary about the wording of the "Hebrew" Bible (the Old Testament), we're speaking about a particular Canaanite dialect.

When Israel's prophets and scribes recorded the sacred prophesies, they wrote them down in Hebrew. As you might imagine, the Jewish people have always venerated Hebrew as a holy language, and they have devoutly maintained it to the present day as the language of choice for use in the services of the Jewish synagogues. Without a doubt, then, we can assume that the people of Christ's day used Hebrew in their religious services. However, that doesn't necessarily mean that they spoke Hebrew in their homes.

The Babylonian captivity of the Jews, which began in 605 B.C., had a profound effect upon them, influencing even their attitude toward Hebrew. They continued to treasure their biblical writings, but during their lengthy exile, they learned the language of their conquerors, which was Chaldean, one of the Aramaic dialects of that time. (Nebuchadnezzar and his dynasty were members of the Chaldean branch of the Aramaeans). So, when the Jews returned to Palestine after their long stay in Mesopotamia, they came back as speakers of the language known as Aramaic, and because they adopted this language as their own and used it for several centuries after their return from exile, Christ and His disciples must have known and used it too.

However, the language situation in Palestine during the time of Christ and the centuries immediately following His time on earth appears to have become even more complicated than what I've described so far. Here's why.

When the Persian armies under the leadership of Cyrus conquered the Babylonian Empire, the Persian rulers adopted and used Aramaic because so many people throughout the Middle East knew and used this language. But when, under Alexander the Great, the Greeks conquered the Persians, the Greek language rapidly became popular among people everywhere in the Middle East. They used it in everyday speech, and it soon became the language of diplomacy, of commerce, of entertainment, of talk on the street, and of almost every other type of communication outside of the home. Even the Jews in Palestine conducted their business transactions in Greek, and they spoke it in their shops and in their fields.

So, the language situation in Palestine during the time of Christ is probably best described as follows: First, the ancient Hebrew language, a variety of Canaanite, continued to hold a venerated place in the thinking of the Jewish people. It was, after all, the language Moses and the prophets used to record and preserve for later generations the Jewish sacred writings. The priests and the teachers (the rabbis) and the various other specialists in the Jewish religion of that period were expected to learn to read the Hebrew writings. However, even though this language was widely used in the texts and prayers of the Jewish religious services, it is highly doubtful that the common people of that day understood much of it. As they became comfortable speaking Aramaic, their ability to understand Hebrew drifted away from them.

Second, the common people of Christ's day probably used Aramaic as their "house" or "home" language—the language they learned from babyhood up and then spoke within their families. It was the language used by the children and the women of the household.

Third, on the streets of the cities, the *Koinē* ("common") dialect of Greek was the language of the day. It was the language of commerce and of men everywhere, though some educated women doubtless knew it too.

Fourth, Latin, the native language of the Romans, was probably not widely used in Palestine during the first century A.D. Of course, because it was the legal language of the empire, Roman functionaries had to use it in official communications. But even the Romans appear to have been accustomed to using Koinē Greek for most of their communication.

During Jesus' ministry, He probably used mostly the Koinē Greek language.

In short, then, it appears that the language most prevalent in Palestine at the time of Christ was Koinē Greek, a common dialect of the Greek language.

A few biblical scholars rather firmly reject the idea that Jesus and His disciples spoke Greek, asserting instead that they knew and spoke only Aramaic. But three basic arguments undergird the belief that Jesus must have spoken Koinē Greek. First, a group of secular documents has been unearthed that provide us with a record of all sorts of relationships and transactions. There are numerous contracts and agreements, ranging from simple wedding summaries to complicated real estate transactions. Some documents deal with the manumission of slaves, and others are lists of shipped goods. There are even all kinds of personal letters, including both messages from young people to their parents and letters between business partners.

For the most part, the messages recorded two or three centuries before Christ were written in Aramaic, but almost without exception, the documents from the first century A.D. and later were written in Greek. They stand as vivid witnesses to the fact that by the time of Christ, communication in Bible lands had very largely shifted from Aramaic to the Koinē dialect of Greek—in fact, that was true not only of the people who lived in Palestine, but also of almost everyone else in the Mediterranean world.

The second evidence that Greek was the language of Christ and His disciples arises from the fact that a number of New Testament sayings have no significant meaning unless they're interpreted as having been originally spoken or composed in Greek. We say things that would be meaningless or, worse, extremely misleading, if taken literally and translated word for word into another language—for instance, "she got it straight from the horse's mouth." There are a number of passages like this in the New Testament, passages that can be understood and interpreted correctly only when the interpreter recognizes their Greek origin. In the chapters that follow, we'll see some interesting examples of this point.

Third, there are a few instances in the Gospel accounts in which Christ's words are recorded in Aramaic. These are significant because they reveal times when our Lord *did* speak in Aramaic. But the point is that these occasions were so unusual and so noteworthy that the Gospel writers felt they should record the exact words that Jesus spoke.

For example, Mark 5:41 tells the story of Jesus' resurrection of a little girl. The Gospel says that when Jesus called her back to life, He uttered the Aramaic words *talitha koum,* "Little girl, rise up." Mark recounts these Aramaic words as if Jesus' use of them was quite out of the ordinary. Actually, it was indeed noteworthy, because it portrays Jesus' concern for the little girl: when our Lord called her back to life, He used the familiar language of the home, not of the street, shop, and field—language that would be comfortable for the awakened child to hear in such a setting.

These three considerations, then, have led most New Testament scholars to conclude that during the three and a half years of Jesus' ministry, He probably used mostly the Koinē Greek language, though they would also agree that there were a few times when He may well have read from the ancient Hebrew scrolls,[1] and New Testament scholars would further agree that on certain occasions, such as in a moment of extreme mental agony on the cross (Mark 15:34), our Lord also spoke Aramaic.

In the following chapters, we will look at a number of passages that must be interpreted in the light of the original Greek manuscripts. A consideration of the Koinē wording of the ancient texts will clarify many of these challenging passages, making them become more meaningful.

---

1. Jesus' familiarity with Hebrew disconcerted His adversaries on at least one occasion. Apparently surprised that He could read Hebrew, one of them asked, "How does this Man know letters, having never studied [them]?" (John 7:15, NKJV).

CHAPTER 2

God's New Kind of Love

Love comes in different forms or grades or intensities. Many languages recognize such distinctions. English, for instance, has words that run the gamut of emotions from *to love* through *to like, to feel affection toward,* through *to appreciate,* and on. People who spoke Koinē Greek—including the writers of the New Testament—made similar distinctions, although theirs don't necessarily coincide precisely with the terms we English speakers use to translate them. We need to consider here three families of Greek words that are translated *love* in English.

- *eros* (a noun): erotic, or sexual, love
- *phileō* (a verb): to naturally like, to naturally be fond of, to be affectionate toward
- *agapaō* (a verb): to place a high value on someone or something

We can ignore *eros,* the first of these three types of love, because the New Testament never uses that Greek word. But the biblical writings do contain references to the other two varieties of love; and it's important that we understand what they mean and how they're used.

The verb *phileō* was employed to depict an emotion that arises naturally. For example, parents typically would (or should) feel this emotional attraction for their own children, and children might be expected to respond to their parents with the same emotion. *Phileō* also includes what sweethearts, spouses, and close companions feel for each other. In many ways, then, we should think of the Greek term *phileō* as being close in meaning to the English verb *to like;* but in a general way it also corresponds to most of the other feelings we have in mind when we use the English word *love.*

This word *love* is also the English term most frequently used to translate the last of the three Greek terms, the verb *agapaō* and the related noun *agapē.* But these words appear to have meant considerably more to the Greeks than the English word *love* generally does to those who speak English. In the first place, we should note that Greek-speaking people didn't use these words very often before Jesus came. It also may be true that because these words were rather rare, most of the people who lived in Palestine, for whom Greek was a second language, may not have understood them until Jesus' teachings and example revealed what He meant by them.

The love Jesus spoke of seems to have primarily meant holding the loved object or person in high regard, considering them to have great value. So, when the Savior spoke of the great regard that we should have for our Creator, He used forms of *agapē/agapaō.* Jesus expanded the depth of this emotion, saying it should involve our whole being—our entire mind, soul, and body (see Matthew 22:37). He said that we should have no less of this kind of love for our fellow human beings than we have for ourselves (verse 39). And in His sermon on the mount, Jesus made the rather shocking statement that we should have this love even for our enemies (Matthew 5:44).

Jesus wasn't saying that we should work ourselves up to feeling sentimental toward our enemies so we

AGAPAŌ:

to place a high value on someone or something

could say that we *liked* them. Rather, He was saying that we should view them as human beings who have as high a value in God's sight as we ourselves do—because, after all, our enemies—even those who persecute us—have the same potential as we have of becoming royal children of the King of the universe. The apostle Paul proved this. Though at first he was a mighty persecutor of God's people, God transformed him into the foremost evangelist of that time.

Christ's teaching about love must have sounded amazingly new and amazingly strange when He first preached it. What He said about it has enlarged our understanding of how we should treat other people. Making use of a relatively unfamiliar word, He blessed it with new meaning. Jesus told His disciples that His plan involved a "new commandment" (John 13:34). Perhaps some of the newness of that commandment—which says that we should "love [*agapaō*] one another"—is derived from the new kind of love He was introducing.

We don't have to do much searching of the Bible to realize that God has placed the main emphasis of the entire

New Testament on this new concept of love. It surely is the very heart of the Christian way of life as taught by Jesus Himself and as amplified by the apostles. Consider, for example, the apostle Paul's description of *agapē* in 1 Corinthians 13, and the apostle John's declaration that the person who doesn't love (*agapaō*) "does not know God" (1 John 4:8). In fact, John 3:16 tells us that God the Father loves the world with *agapē* love.

John 21:15ff contains an interesting story in which John uses the words *agapaō* and its less-demanding synonym *phileō*, revealing something of the nuances these terms have. The passage relates a verbal interchange between Jesus and the disciple Peter that took place shortly after Jesus' resurrection.

Jesus began by asking the disciple who had denied Him, "Simon son of John, do you love [*agapaō*] me more than these?" (In other words, "Do you love Me more that these other disciples do?") This question opened the door for Peter to try to compensate for his denial by declaring the superiority of his love. But Peter didn't boast. Instead, he simply and humbly replied, "Yes, Lord, You know that I *like* [*phileō*] You" (or "I'm fond of You"; "I care about You," John 21:15; author's translation).

The Lord probed again, asking Peter a second time, "Simon son of John, do you love [*agapaō*] me?" (verse 16). Again Peter refrained from boasting about the depths of his love—the superior love that Jesus had spoken so much about. Instead, he humbly replied, "Yes, Lord, You know that I *like* [*phileō*] You" (verse 16; author's translation).

Then Jesus added an interesting emotional twist by changing His query. Picking up on Peter's answers, He asked, "Do you *like* [*phileō*] Me?" (verse 17; author's translation). It's as though He were saying, "All right, you've made no claim to have the lofty kind of love. Are you really My friend?" The implication seems to be, "Would someone who truly is My friend deny Me?"

The Gospel tells us that Peter was "grieved" because Jesus said the third time, "Do you *phileō* Me?" We can hear Peter sobbing in distress as he protests, "Lord, You know all things; You know that I *phileō* You." While he couldn't claim to have attained the divine love, he could at least profess the regard he felt for his Savior as conveyed by the less-demanding term.

The ancient Greek documents of the Gospel of John clearly distinguish the two verbs, but most modern English translations gloss over the difference, translating both with the word *love*. One wonders why. The Gospel writer purposely told us the words Christ spoke to Peter and how he responded, and the subtle implications of the distinctly different verbs add meaning and depth to the story.

We can conclude that when the word *love* appears in the Gospels (especially in the words of Christ), the Greek original is almost without exception the verb *agapaō* or the related noun. The same is true in 1 John, and of course, the love Paul praised in 1 Corinthians 13 is *agapē* love. By using these terms, Jesus, the Gospel writers, and Paul evidently were all trying to teach the world the essence of the divine kind of love, God's love.

CHAPTER 4

John 3:16—Beloved,
but Misunderstood

John 3:16 is the Bible's most frequently quoted verse, its most memorized text, its most encouraging scripture, its best-known passage, its most beloved selection. This verse, as commonly interpreted, has blessed millions by pointing out the immensity of God's love for the human race. Yet it is without a doubt the most widely misunderstood verse in the entire Bible. Understanding its full meaning can awaken an even greater appreciation of God's love.

Before we get into the matter of the mistranslation, let me briefly point out that this verse says God gave His Son because He loved (*agapaō*) the people of this world. As I explained in a preceding chapter of this book, to love with an *agapaō* kind of love means to place a high value on whatever it is that the person loves. In other words, John 3:16 tells us that God the Father gave His Son because He considers the rebel children of Adam to be of great value—in fact, of such great value as to be worth His Son's crucifixion! Such a realization is in itself enough to make John 3:16 an amazing scripture.

However, this beloved verse contains an element that

has been badly rendered in Bible translations ranging from the King James Version through nearly all the modern versions.[1] The word that has been mistranslated so often is the Greek adverb *houtōs,* which translators have generally rendered as "so." However, in this case it doesn't actually mean "so," even though, indirectly, it does say a great deal about how much God must have loved the world. A proper understanding of the meaning of this adverb makes John 3:16 an even more exciting verse to think about and to preach about!

At this point I'm going to use a few technical terms. Don't let them scare you off—I'll tell you plainly what they mean, and what meaning they add to our understanding of John 3:16! The Greek word *houtōs* is an *anaphoric deictic*

HOUTŌS:

so—"in the way I just pointed out"

adverb. Does that sound like gibberish? Let's break it down. First, this word is an *adverb,* which simply means that it tells us how the action of the main verb ("loved") in the sentence was done. Second, it's a *deictic* word—which means that it's a word that calls attention to or emphasizes something. Here, it means something like "in *this* way." And third, it's an *anaphoric* word, which means that it refers *back* to something that was mentioned previously. *An anaphoric word does not point forward, as the translation "so" seems to suggest.*

To render the original Greek correctly, then, we need a word that tells us how an action was done while simultaneously emphasizing that action and referring the reader back to

---

1. A recent edition of the Holman Study Bible does offer a suitable translation of this important verse.

the preceding context. Unfortunately, the English language doesn't have a word that by itself can neatly capture what the Greek word *houtōs* says here. Any translator who wishes to convey everything that *houtōs* means here has to use several words or phrases. Expanded in this way, the text reads something like this paraphrase: "God loved the world in the very way I've been talking about, which is why He gave His Son . . . ," etc.

In other words, when Jesus used the adverb *houtōs* in this verse, He wasn't trying to emphasize *how much* God loved us. That's certainly a good thing to emphasize, but it wasn't His point here. Rather, Jesus was telling Nicodemus that God loved us *in the particular way Jesus had talked about in the previous verses.* This means that if we want to translate John 3:16 correctly—if we want to see the complete picture of God's love for the world—we must first catch Jesus' point in John 3:14 and 15. And what makes the whole question so astonishing, so gripping, is the fact that verses 14 and 15 contain one of the most amazing illustrations in the entire Bible! Those critical verses picture Jesus as reminding Nicodemus of a strange episode that occurred as Moses was leading the Israelites of old through the wilderness on their way to the Promised Land.[2]

According to Numbers 21, the people of Israel were bitterly and rebelliously complaining against Moses and even against God because of the difficulties the journey entailed— specifically, because of the scanty supplies of food and water. Scripture says God sent "fiery serpents" among the people—poisonous snakes that bit many of them, killing quite a few. Coming to their senses, the people repented of

---

2. Numbers 21 contains the complete story—see especially verses 4–9.

their sinful complaining and begged Moses to do something to rescue them, which he does—he prays.

At this point the story takes an astonishing turn: God tells Moses to make an image of a fiery serpent and fasten it to a pole. And when people who were bitten looked to this image of evil, they were healed. They didn't die.

Astonishingly, Jesus used this ancient story to illustrate how He would rescue us sinful human beings from the consequences of our sinful rebellion against God. He told Nicodemus that Christ would be raised up *in the same way* that Moses lifted up the image of the evil, fiery serpent. In fact, this was just another way in which God the Father and Jesus the Son could say in a memorable way that when Jesus came to destroy the power of sin, He came in the form of sinful humanity. Isaiah prophesied that God's special Servant would be "numbered with the transgressors" (Isaiah 53:12). In other words, even though He hadn't sinned, He would be treated as a sinner. It's also what Paul meant when he said that Jesus, the One who knew no sin, *was made to be sin* for our sakes (2 Corinthians 5:21).

Jesus told Nicodemus that just as Moses "lifted up" the repulsive snake so people could look upon it, so our Lord was to be lifted up and made into a public spectacle—as though He were a despicable transgressor. In the Roman Empire, punishment by crucifixion was viewed as being the worst of all forms of execution, so it was reserved for the most wicked criminals. By crucifying Christ, then, the Roman and Jewish authorities were in effect proclaiming to the world that He was the most loathsome and wicked wretch that humankind could imagine.

It is in the light of the horrible illustration from Moses' day, which Jesus applied to Himself in John 3:14, 15, that the words of Jesus recorded in John 3:16 places before us God's remedy for sin. In this beloved verse He declares, as paraphrased here, "It was in *this way*—by giving His Son to be raised on a cross like the serpent on the pole—that God loved the world: His love compelled Him to send His Son to be crucified, to be raised on a cross so that whoever believes in Him will not perish but will have everlasting life."

It was in this way that God loved you and me. He gave His Son to suffer the sinner's fate in your place and mine so that we don't have to perish but can have eternal life! What astonishing love! How could we turn away from Someone who values us so much? The only appropriate response to such love is to give ourselves fully and completely to Him for eternity.

CHAPTER 5

The Least in the Kingdom

In the previous chapter, we saw that a correct translation of the adverb *houtōs* in John 3:16 expands the meaning of that verse. Is this adverb used elsewhere in the New Testament, and if so, can we find additional meaning in those other verses too? The answer to both questions is Yes.

While the correct translation of those other verses may not add as much to their meaning as it does in the case in John 3:16, many of them do contain addi-

Matthew 5:19: "Called least in the kingdom of heaven."

tional thoughts that typically are minimized or at times even overlooked in most of the current Bible translations. In the paragraphs that follow, I examine several of these passages in order to illustrate the interesting possibilities they contain. As you read them, notice that the thought they were intended to convey seems to stand out more vividly when we remember that in most cases *houtōs* is meant to draw our attention back to the context of the preceding verse or verses. This adverb emphasizes how much some current thing or experience resembles something similar in the past.

- **Matthew 5:12.** "Blessed are ye, when men shall revile you, and persecute you, and shall say all manner of evil against you falsely, for my sake. Rejoice, and be exceeding glad: for great is your reward in heaven: for *so* persecuted they the prophets which were before you" (verses 11, 12, KJV; emphasis added).

    Here, Jesus told His followers to *expect* persecution because people had treated the Old Testament prophets in the same way [*houtōs*] they were being treated. The *houtōs* likens the treatment of the prophets mentioned in verse 12 to the contemporary persecution Jesus spoke of in verse 11.

    In other words, Jesus was saying that persecution wasn't evidence that God had forsaken them. Far from it! In fact, persecution was evidence that like the prophets of old, they were troubling the enemy.

- **Matthew 5:19.** "Whosoever therefore shall break one of these least commandments, and shall teach men *so* [i.e., teach men to, like them, relax the "minor" commandments], he shall be called the least in the kingdom of heaven" (KJV; emphasis added).

    In both Matthew 5:12 and 5:19, the King James Version and the Revised Standard Version translate *houtōs* simply as *so*—a rendering that doesn't convey as strongly as *houtōs* the comparison that is intended between the current clause and the previous one.

- **Matthew 9:33.** "And when the devil was cast out, the dumb spake: and the multitudes marvelled, saying, It was never *so* seen in Israel" (KJV; emphasis added). The people who witnessed the Lord's miraculous casting out of a demon exclaimed in astonishment something to the effect of "nothing like this happened in the old days." Some modern versions combine the negative word with their rendering of this word and give the whole thought as "never." However, such a rendering essentially omits a real comparison between what Jesus did and what happened in the past.

- **Matthew 12:40.** "For as Jonas was three days and three nights in the whale's belly; *so* shall the Son of man be three days and three nights in the heart of the earth" (KJV; emphasis added). In this verse, Christ compares what He must yet experience to something that happened in the past. He declared that His burial in the tomb for three days would in some way *be just like* Jonah's burial at sea. So, the passage should say, "Because just as Jonah was in the belly of the whale for three days and for three nights, *in the same way* the Son of man will be in the heart of the earth for three days and for three nights." However, the King James Version and a number of other translations render this interesting adverb with the ambiguous word *so* and thereby miss the exact thought of this verse.

By rendering *houtōs* as *so* in a few passages, such as those mentioned above, various translations may not only seem somewhat ambiguous, they may actually miss some of the meaning of a passage. This is true because the term *so* is easily confused with such terms as *therefore* and *hence* and the like, a meaning that the English *so* possesses at times. However, by looking closely at the original wording, students of the Scriptures can easily determine more exactly the meaning of the text they are considering.

The King James Version's rendering of Matthew 24:33, "So likewise ye, when ye shall see all these things, know that it is near, even at the doors," illustrates this point. Influenced by the various meanings of the English *so,* people may read this word at the beginning of the verse as meaning "therefore" or "hence." But this verse is actually reminding us to view the signs we see of Christ's nearing advent *in the same way* that the previous verse says we read the signs in nature that tell us summer is approaching. Thus Matthew 24:33 could be more accurately viewed as saying something like "in the same way [that you determine the approach of summer], when you see all these things [i.e., the signs that precede the advent of Christ], you can determine that He is near, even at the doors."

To locate other passages of the Bible in which *houtōs* has been translated somewhat ambiguously, you can consult exhaustive concordances such as *Young's Analytical Concordance to the Bible* and *Strong's Exhaustive Concordance of the Bible.* These concordances reveal that the word *houtōs* has been rendered as *so* more than 150 times in the King James Version of the Bible. You'll find stronger emphases and more energy in many of these passages if you'll render *houtōs* more clearly.

CHAPTER 6

The Right Thing, the Wrong Reason

Our spiritual advisors often admonish us to study the Bible. They, of course, know that daily attention to the words of Scripture strengthens our relationship with God and helps to develop healthy Christian characters. As we journey toward the heavenly kingdom, we need the gentle but strong influence that regular Bible study has upon us.

Many of those who promote the reading of Scripture quote the King James Version's translation of John 5:39 as supporting this commendable practice. In that version, the verse begins with the words, "Search the scriptures"—a useful admonition because an active searching of the Bible that challenges our minds is much more interesting than is a mere nebulous, undirected reading.

Ironically, a careful look at the wording of John 5:39 provides a highly instructive example of what we can learn by actually *searching* the Bible—by studying its contents thoroughly. When we give that kind of attention to this verse, we find that in the original Greek, the first word is ambiguous. The Greek word translated in the King James Version as *search* is a form of the verb *eraunaō*. Unfortunately, the form this word has in this verse—the way it's spelled and accented—fits both the *imperative* and the *declarative* "moods." (Hang in there—this isn't as technical as it may seem!) What you need to know here is that verbs in the imperative mood give commands, and verbs in the declarative mood make statements—they simply say what's happening. So, if Jesus spoke the word as an imperative, He was saying, "Search the scriptures because . . ." etc., but if He spoke it as a declarative, He was saying, "You search the scriptures because . . ." etc.

ERAUNAŌ:

search; examine;

investigate

The men who produced the King James Version chose to translate this verb as an imperative—as though Jesus were commanding the leaders of the Jews to search the Scriptures. But the original Greek word could just as well have been translated as a declarative, which would mean that Jesus was simply stating what those who were opposing Him were doing.

Since the critical word here is so ambiguous, how can we determine which meaning is correct?

The answer is that the context should tell us what Jesus actually said—unless the context itself is also ambiguous.

In this case, it isn't. In fact, it's quite clear. Although the first seventeen verses of John 5 set the stage fully, what we really need to know begins with verse 18. There we are told that the Jews—essentially, those who were the *leaders* of the Jews at that time—were looking for a way to put Christ to death because they resented His teachings. The verse we're seeking to understand, John 5:39, comes two-thirds of the way through Christ's rather lengthy response to their plotting (John 5:19–47). This context makes it quite obvious which mood of the verb He was likely to have used.

It's quite improbable that in this situation Jesus would have been urging the leaders of the Jews to search the Scriptures of that time, the Old Testament. They already were doing that. In fact, they took great pride in how well they knew those sacred writings. So, it's more likely that Christ was acknowledging their ongoing searches of the Scriptures—and pointing out that despite their study, they were missing the most important point those sacred writings make—that He is the Son of God and the only source of eternal life. The correct translation of John 5:39, 40, then, reads something like this: "You are searching the Scriptures because you think you have eternal life in them. These [writings] bear witness about Me, but you don't come to Me to obtain life."

While Christ was saying the Jewish leaders were missing an essential part of the Scripture they were studying, He was also, in a sense, commending the study of Scripture. In that sense, we, too, can hear in this verse Christ instructing us that we should be engaged in frequent "searches" of the divine Word for our own spiritual growth. But we mustn't miss the primary point in this important passage. It's the point that Christ Himself made about the reason *why* searching the Scripture is valuable. This practice is valuable because these writings testify about Christ, the coming Savior of lost humanity. In other words, if we search Scripture carefully—even the Old Testament—we can find in it hidden testimonies about the Son of God Himself. And Jesus' remark to the Jewish leaders tells us that He *wants* us to find these evidences for ourselves.

How can we find them?

Some of them are rather obvious. For example, immediately after the sin of Adam and Eve, God promised them the coming of a "Seed," a "Descendant," who would "bruise" the head of the serpent (Genesis 3:15). Through Moses, God gave another prophetic message regarding an important Personage who was to come: "The LORD your God will raise up for you a prophet like me [Moses] from among your own people; you shall heed such a prophet" (Deuteronomy 18:15; see also verse 18). And the beautiful extended prophecy of Isaiah 53 is another testimony that seems obviously to point to the coming of the Savior.

In another prophetic message, God told Daniel about a Messiah who was to come at the end of a lengthy period, each day of which represented a literal year (Daniel 9:24, 25). In the same prophetic message, God said this Messiah would be "cut off," and in the middle of a mysterious week, He would "make sacrifice and offering cease" (verses 26, 27). Obviously, this also was an important witness about the coming Messiah.

The various animal sacrifices seem also to have been representations of the great sacrifice that the Son of God made on Calvary. John the Baptist apparently grasped the significance of the symbolism in the ancient sacrificial system, because he introduced Jesus with the words, "Look, here is the Lamb of God!" (John 1:36).

We can uncover a number of these easy-to-identify predictions in the Old Testament by simple searches. Other symbolic testimonies about Christ may be much harder to find, though the search is fascinating. The book of Ruth, for instance, is full of symbolic prophecies about the coming Redeemer (Hebrew, *goel*)—the Person who would serve as the "near-kinsman," with the legal right to buy back the lost family property (here, representing the world) and marry the woman linked to that property (the church). The Song of Solomon may also represent a symbolic portrayal of the coming Messiah.

In a number of places, then, the Old Testament bears witness to Christ. Of these Scriptures He said, "It is they that testify on my behalf" (John 5:39). Apparently, He wants us to search the Bible for the testimonies that point to Him. Finding and applying the truths of God's Word will strengthen our spiritual life and prepare us for Christ's return.

CHAPTER 7

The Judge and the Dangerous Widow

The story itself is fascinating, and it speaks to us because Jesus applied its moral directly to the spiritual situation of those who live in the time just before He returns. Yet two of the most important and interesting parts of this story of "The Dangerous Widow" are seldom mentioned. Many of the scholars who have attempted to analyze the episode even miss them.

The story, recorded in Luke 18:1–8, features two main characters and alludes to at least one other person. Jesus said a certain widow was involved in a dispute with an opponent, whom He didn't name. The wording of the Greek text indicates that the widow felt this adversary of hers should be brought to justice by the legal system and forced to grant her claim. Apparently, she must have felt that this other party had seriously mistreated her.

So the widow repeatedly brought her charges before a judge in her city, demanding that justice be done. But this official was an "unjust judge"—a man who neither feared God nor cared about his fellow human beings (see verse 2).

He simply wasn't interested in justice in general or in her case in particular.

But the widow wasn't one to be easily put off. She persisted in her pursuit of justice, raising her case before the judge again and again. It seems that these two people may have eventually gotten into a battle of wills—the widow almost more interested in vindication, in being declared right, than in whatever material reward winning the case might have brought her; and the judge, though not caring where justice lay, refusing to pursue the matter out of sheer stubbornness. He didn't want to cave in to the woman's demands, whether or not they were justified. As we read or hear the story, we can't be blamed for wondering just which one would yield first!

HUPŌPIAZŌ:

strike under the eye; give a black eye

Ultimately, it was the unjust judge who gave in. A literal translation of the Greek text reads: "Afterward, he said within himself, 'Even though I do not fear God nor do I respect man, since this widow is constantly bothering me, I will avenge her, lest she run out of [patience] and give me a black eye!' " (Luke 18:4, 5; author's translation). The last five words of this quotation are translated from the Greek word *hupōpiazō*, a word that comes from the sport of prize-fighting! In other words, the original text implies that the unjust judge became afraid that this woman, who was so tenacious and demanding, might eventually lose her temper and attack him physically! To save himself the pain and perhaps embarrassment that would bring, he finally decided to go along with her petition and bring her adversary to justice.

The intent of the parable seems clear. In it, Christ was presenting a distinct contrast: picturing on one hand a hard-hearted judge who would show mercy to a begging widow only *after* he decided she might resort to physical violence if he waited any longer, and on the other, our loving and deeply interested heavenly Parent, who is happy to listen to our requests because He cares about us and takes pleasure in providing for our needs. In fact, God has demonstrated His love and care for us by even giving His own Son to *die* for us, and, as the apostle Paul has assured us, "He who did not withhold his own Son, but gave him up for all of us, will he not with him also give us everything else?" (Romans 8:32). How different God is from the unjust judge!

But when Jesus told this story, He concluded it by adding a heart-searching application of it to the people living just before His second coming. In the King James Version, the added line reads: "Nevertheless when the Son of man cometh, shall he find faith on the earth?" (Luke 18:8). Unfortunately, this translation isn't complete. The original Greek has a small word that most translations seem to ignore. This word, *ara,* is a grammatical term that indicates that the question is to be answered with a No.

So there's a great contrast between the parable and the question with which Jesus ends it. The parable looks at God and consequently is strongly positive: unlike corrupt human judges whose only concern is their convenience, our heavenly Adjudicator gladly works in behalf of His chosen ones, ruling in their favor and condemning their adversary. But Jesus' question, on the other hand, is focused on human beings—which explains the sad and pessimistic conclusion. Jesus wonders whether at the end of history God will be able to find *anyone* who still has faith.

The call that this parable implicitly voices is that *each one of us must not disappoint Him at a time when faith will be in short supply*—so scarce, in fact, that one might think that it is just no longer to be found here. As children of the heavenly King, we must continually look to Him so our faith will be strong when everyone else has given it up. This seems to be our Lord's primary point in His story of the dangerous widow.

CHAPTER 8

Did Jesus *Really* Call Her
a *Dog?*

There were times during Jesus' ministry when He seemed to have felt especially compelled to make unexpected side trips—instances when He deviated from His plans in order to care for needs that He would have missed if He had adhered too closely to His usual itinerary.

John 4:4 seems to refer to one such occurrence. The King James Version has the Gospel writer saying, "he must needs go through Samaria." In modern English the wording of the ancient manuscripts might be phrased something like this: "He just *had* to go through Samaria."

Jesus was in Judea, and He wanted to go to Galilee. He didn't actually have to go through Samaria to get from the one place to the other—there were other routes, and, in fact, most Jews who made that trip chose one of those other routes because they despised the Samaritans. Why then did Jesus feel that He "had" to go through Samaria? Because He knew there was a Samaritan woman—and, in fact, a whole village full of Samaritans—who needed His ministry, who needed to hear the words of life He came to share.

However, this chapter focuses on another example of the Savior's choosing to go somewhere unusual. In Matthew 15:21, the Master is described as taking a special trip far to the north of Judea, north even of Galilee, to the heathen cities of Tyre and Sidon. Again, Jesus knew what He was doing and why. He knew that in that territory, far from the region where He spent most of His time, there was a woman—called a Canaanite in Matthew 15:22 and a Syro-Phoenician in Mark 7:26—who desperately needed Him to heal her daughter, who was demon-possessed. It seems Jesus thought this a prime opportunity to teach a lesson to His disciples too—that He was the Savior and Healer not only of the people of Israel but of the other nations as well.

Jesus chose an unusual way to illumine the minds of the Twelve. At first, upon meeting the woman, He acted the way a typical rabbi might—He ignored the woman, projecting an attitude of aloofness that the disciples no doubt thought quite normal and justified.

When the woman continued to plead for Jesus' help, He replied with words that, as reported in most of our Bible versions, seem harsh and unsympathetic—completely out of character for Jesus as we know Him: "It is not fair to take the children's food and throw it to the dogs" (Matthew 15:26).

The disciples would have felt in total harmony with the cold rebuff these words convey. That heathen woman could expect no sympathy from them. In their minds, their Master's wonderful works were all reserved for the people who worshiped the true God. Other people could and should be referred to as dogs—that they were unclean and undeserving was simply their tough luck.

However, the original Greek doesn't say Jesus called this woman a dog. The word He used is actually *kunarion,* a term that denoted puppies and pet dogs rather than the street dogs that were regarded with such disdain.

It seems likely that if Jesus had actually called that woman—a heathen and a foreigner—a dog in the full negativity of the term, she would have felt totally rejected, turned away sadly, and gone home without making further efforts to get His help. But a puppy? A pet? This term gives a different nuance to the conversation. In using it, Jesus provided that Gentile woman with a convenient steppingstone to faith.

KUNARION:

little dog; house dog;

lap dog

Although dogs were usually considered to be dirty scavengers and so were generally excluded from the home, children were sometimes allowed to keep puppies as pets. And as pets, puppies often received warm, loving care. So, when Jesus slipped in the word *puppies,* the desperate mother He was speaking to immediately took that as an indication that He might look favorably upon her petition. So, she agreed with Jesus that the puppies shouldn't be given the food meant for the children of the family—yet, she said, people let the puppies eat the crumbs that fall from the table.

Her response was, of course, what the Lord was hoping for. He wanted her to press on in faith and not to be discouraged—that's why He had made the way easier for her by moderating what otherwise would have been harsh, repulsive language. So the woman was encouraged in her faith, her daughter was freed, and the disciples learned that

God's blessings were meant for the Gentile races as well as for the Jews.

But in this story there's the hint of another lesson for the rest of us. It is this—that God has given us all wonderfully rich promises. To be sure, He hasn't necessarily promised to provide us with rich cushions of wealth and fame (though occasionally we may have these), but He *has* promised us His active interest in even the temporal and physical parts of our lives. We do well, then, not to give up our efforts to seek His help in the matters that concern us. If this story tells us anything, it tells us that we have every right to look for the steppingstones that God has placed here and there as subtle encouragement for us to come to Him and plead our cases. We need to be persistent in our prayers to God.

Jesus agreed that even the puppies have a right to the crumbs that fall off the master's table—and because we are of far greater worth than puppies, we should eagerly and confidently make our petitions known to our Father in heaven. And in pressing our petitions upon Him, we have the right to look for steppingstones for our faith—the many promises in the Word of God that tell us He's interested in the things that concern us.

CHAPTER 9

Between a Rock and a Stone

Among the plays on words to be found in the New Testament, the one in Matthew 16:18 is probably the best known. Christ originated this particular wordplay, basing it on Simon Peter's name. Some churches—the Roman Catholic Church among them—teach that Christ used it to proclaim Peter to be the rock on which He would build His church. Then, claiming that Peter belonged to their communion, they say this all indicates their church to be God's true church.

Before we look at the wordplay, we'll look at its setting. The story begins with Christ asking His disciples who the people around them were saying He was. When they had answered that question, He asked them, "Who do *you* say that I am?" (Matthew 16:15; emphasis added). Peter answered the question boldly: "You are the Messiah, the Son of the living God" (verse 16).

Christ commended Peter for his answer: "Blessed are you, Simon son of Jonah! For flesh and blood has not revealed this to you, but my Father in heaven" (verse 17). Then He made an important point by contrasting a pair of words. He said, "I tell you, you are Peter, and on this rock I will build my church, and the gates of Hades will not prevail against it" (verse 18). In this verse, Christ contrasted the great truth Peter had spoken in his confession of faith, on the one hand, with the significance of his name on the other. *Peter*[1] (*Petros* in the Koinē Greek) denoted a rock—a stone small enough that a man could pick it up in one hand. But Christ didn't say He would build His church upon a *petros*. He said He would build it upon a *petra*—a word primarily used of large rocks: the rocky stratum that made a good foundation for a house (see Matthew 7:24); a rock wall large enough that a tomb could be carved into it; a rocky cliff.

PETROS:
a stone

So, Christ's reply to Peter could be appropriately translated as follows: "You are *Petros* [a stone], but I will build my church upon a massive rock [*petra*]." In other words, in His reply, our Lord used a play

PETRA:
rock

on words to make what He said memorable. He was contrasting the flesh-and-blood man Peter (*petros*), a relatively small stone, with the great truth (the *petra*) that Peter had voiced—that Jesus was the Christ, "the Son of the living God."

Theologians who want to support the claim that Peter was the rock on which Christ is building His church—that he was the first pope—have attempted to discount the contrast between the two Greek words by claiming that this contrast didn't exist in Aramaic,

---

1. As we can see in Matthew 16:17, *Simon* was actually the given name of this disciple. *Peter* was a nickname.

which, they say was the language that Christ spoke on this occasion.

However, a contrasting pair of words meaning "rock" *does* exist in Aramaic. The proof is as follows: Peter— *Petros,* the "stone"—is also known in the Bible by the Aramaic name *Kephas* (rendered as "Cephas" in many modern versions of the Bible), which means the same thing as does *Petros* (see John 1:40–42). And to find an Aramaic equivalent of *petra,* the massive rock, we need only to turn to historians and archeologists, who tell us that the ancient capital city of the Edomites was known at one time by the Aramaic name *Sela* and later by the Greek name *Petra*. This capital of the kingdom of Edom derived its name (both in Aramaic and in Greek) from the fact that it was located among rocky massifs. In fact, some of the houses and even the public buildings of this ancient city were carved out of these huge rock walls. Even today this ancient city is known to tourists as the city of rock.

So, like Greek, the Aramaic language did have a pair of words that meant "rock," one of which, *kephas,* meant a small rock—a stone—while the other, *petra,* meant a rock big enough to be the foundation and even the entire structure of a large building. However, as I pointed out in chapter 1, it is most likely that on this occasion Jesus spoke Greek, the common language of the day, and it's in the Greek originals of Scripture that we find this beautiful example of an ancient play on words.

What does it all mean? Perhaps something to the effect that our confessions of faith that Jesus is the Messiah, the Christ, are valuable, but flesh and blood alone isn't adequate to serve as a foundation for the church

God is building. Another, stronger and more stable Rock will fill that role.[2]

---

2. Other passages of Scripture that also use the term "rock" may be helpful here too—even though they're based on yet another Greek word meaning rock: *lithos*. See, e.g., Romans 9:30–33; 1 Peter 2:4ff.

CHAPTER 10

Watch for *These* Signs

During recent decades, our world has witnessed a distressful increase in both threats of war and actual international wars. Are these not vivid signs that we are living in the very last days of our world's history? Don't preachers frequently tell us to be sure to renew our allegiance to God because the proliferation of warfare warns us of the coming end of time?

A more careful, attentive reading of Christ's descriptive discourse on the Mount of Olives leads us to re-examine the details of the "signs of the times." Such a reading impresses upon us our Lord's statement: "You will hear of wars and rumors of wars; see that you are not alarmed; for this must take place, *but the end is not yet*" (Matthew 24:6; emphasis added). A very literal translation of the original Greek wording may make it emphatically clearer: "You will be constantly hearing

> **Matthew 24:6: "You will hear of wars and rumors of wars; . . . but the end is not yet."**

about wars and reports of wars. Always watch out [so as] not to be alarmed; because it is necessary for [such things] to happen; but the end is not yet!" So warfare alone is not a safe indicator of how close we may be to the end of time.

A careful study of such biblical passages as Matthew 24 should provide us with more reliable insights as to how close we might be to the end of the world. In fact, a literal translation of verse 14 of that chapter does just that for us: "This gospel of the kingdom shall be proclaimed to all nations in the entire inhabited world, and *then* the end will come." Reports of successful evangelism in distant places are a much more reliable indicator of how close we are to the end of time—as are such developments as the increase of the expression of personal anger (see chapter 33 of this book) and the decrease of faith in the Bible's accounts (2 Peter 3:3–7). These all indicate where we are on the time line of the history of this world. When we observe the increase of these notable signs, we have reason to believe that our Lord will return soon.

"Seeing then that all these things shall be dissolved, what manner of persons ought ye to be in all holy conversation and godliness, looking for and hasting unto the coming of the day of God, wherein the heavens being on fire shall be dissolved, and the elements shall melt with fervent heat? Nevertheless we, according to his promise, look for new heavens and a new earth, wherein dwelleth righteousness. Wherefore, beloved, seeing that ye look for such things, be diligent that ye may be found of him in peace, without spot, and blameless" (2 Peter 3:11–14, KJV).

CHAPTER 11

Will Christians "Never See Death"?

One of our most basic instincts pushes us to avoid death at all costs. That we have such a drive is entirely understandable because death means a cessation of our consciousness. When we die, we cease to exist. But, of course, as Christians, we trust our Lord, believing that He has the power to rescue us from this dreaded end. We believe that because He has obtained "the keys of death and the grave" (Revelation 1:18, NLT), He will deliver us from death when He comes again; and that hope assuages our fear and stress and brings us healing comfort.

However, there is one verse of Scripture in which Christ seems to promise believers a greater victory over death than He has delivered. The apostle John reports that He said, "Very truly, I tell you, whoever keeps my word will never see death" (John 8:51). Taken just as it reads, this verse seems to say quite clearly that no one who sincerely follows Jesus will experience death. Yet other than the generations now living, every single follower of Christ *has* died. In fact, even Christ Himself experienced death. Obviously, then, John 8:51 is a problem text—one that demands an explanation. Just what did Jesus mean when He bluntly declared that His followers would never "see death"?

Explaining this puzzling passage doesn't pose as much of a challenge as we might expect. The basic solution is found in the meaning of a single word.

This critical word is the verb translated "see," a word that normally expresses the simple act of noticing or observing something. In this passage, however, the Greek word translated "see" isn't the usual *blepō*, a word that means using one's eyes; instead, the ancient manuscripts employ here quite a different term— *theōreō*, a verb that was often used in contexts that involved a more prolonged or intensive act of observing, often, one motivated by concern.

THEŌREŌ:

look at; observe;

perceive; see

For instance, Matthew used *theōreō* when he wrote that the two Marys "went to *see* the tomb" (Matthew 28:1; emphasis added). Luke says that when they went into the tomb, they were puzzled because Christ's body wasn't there (Luke 24:3, 4), which means it isn't much of a stretch for us to assume that their "seeing" was both thorough and driven by concern— nuances conveyed by the verb *theōreō*.

Luke used this verb in telling the dramatic story of the apostle Paul's escape from shipwreck on his trip to Rome. When Paul and the other survivors come ashore, they gather around a bonfire to recover from the draining experience. But as Paul adds sticks to the fire, a poisonous reptile slides out of the firewood and drives its fangs into his hand. All those watching expect him to die quickly. The King James Version reports that they "looked a great while," but they "saw no harm come to him" (Acts 28:6). Again, their "looking" was no mere quick glance in his direction. They were watching with great interest and concern because they expected him to die at any moment. Fortunately, of course, Paul miraculously survived.

Thus the ancient verb *theōreō* was employed in the New Testament in a number of contexts that, rather than suggesting quick glances, referred to careful observation motivated by concern, or, at times, even by distress. Other examples include

- The unclean spirits who, "when they *saw* him," fell down in defeat before Him (Mark 3:11, KJV; emphasis added).
- The disciples, who when they first saw their resurrected Lord, were overwhelmed with fear because they "thought that they *were seeing* a ghost" (Luke 24:37; emphasis added).
- The hired shepherd, who runs away from the sheep in his care when he *"sees"* a wolf coming (John 10:12; emphasis added).
- The Jewish leaders, who, when they *"saw"* the boldness and effectiveness of Peter's and John's public witnessing put them in prison (Acts 4:13; emphasis added).

In all these contexts where the act of seeing involved concern, the verb employed was *theōreō*. It seems, then, that in using this verb regarding the death of His followers, Christ wasn't saying that they would never be exposed to the sight or the experience of death. All Christians eventually feel its impact—both as it takes away their loved ones and as it strikes themselves. Instead, Christ seems to have used this particular verb to remind Christians that they experience death as well as life differently from the way unbelievers do. Christians are in the hands of a loving God; and when their last day of life comes, they don't have to view death with the concern—the fear—that characterizes those who have rejected Christ, those "who have no hope" (1 Thessalonians 4:13). Because of the resurrection, their life will go on eternally as they enjoy the fulfillment of John 3:16: "everyone who believes in him [will] not perish but may have eternal life." So the statement of Christ recorded in John 8:51 simply means that His followers shouldn't *view* death—shouldn't *see* it—with the same hopelessness as do those people who don't know the One who has the keys to the tomb.

CHAPTER 12

The King's Arrival: Secret or Celebrated?

Historians tell of a special event that took place when ancient Rome ruled the Near East and the Mediterranean world. They say that once an emperor decided to make a state visit to one of the larger cities of his realm. The inhabitants of the city were delighted that the great ruler was going to honor them with a visit. Accordingly, they made extensive preparations to welcome him, cleaning up their city and adorning it beautifully. And on the day of the emperor's arrival, crowds of people lined the roadway so that as he rode toward the city, he was met by a lively and noisy populace that made him feel honored, loved, and welcomed. The inhabitants of the city minted a coin to commemorate their emperor's visit, and for years after, they remembered the day of his arrival.

The emperor's coming to visit his subjects in their home city was called his *parousia*. This Greek word, which appeared on the coin the local officials minted, denoted a "coming," or more specifically, an "arrival."

The Greek expression that was employed by the people of that fortunate city became an important word for Christians, because the writers of the New Testament used it of the coming of their beloved Lord in power and glory to take His people from this world and bring them to the city that will be their home for eternity. (For references in which *parousia*—usually rendered "coming"—occurs, see Matthew 24:3; 24:27, 37, 39; 1 Thessalonians 4:15; 2 Thessalonians 2:1; James 5:7, 8; etc.)

Theologians of a certain persuasion, however, have taken the expression *parousia* somewhat out of context and have viewed it as a technical term that designates the time when, as one of an elaborate series of events at the end of the age, Jesus will secretly "rapture" His saints out of this world.

Those who look for Jesus' return should be sure they understand clearly what the writers of the New Testament meant when they used the term *parousia*. Those who investigate how the word was used in the time and place in which the New Testament was written will find that it was used to describe the emperor's *coming to* or *arrival at* an honored city. It didn't connote a secret event, but rather an observable, public happening.

PAROUSIA:

a coming; an arrival

On one occasion, the twelve disciples asked Jesus what "sign" would mark the twin events that they referred to as "Your coming" (the *parousia*) and "the end of the age/world." In their question they employed a unique construction that bound the two nouns together in one unit, suggesting that they realized that the *parousia* and the end were essentially *one* event.

As reported in Matthew 24, Mark 13, and Luke 21, in answer to their question, our Lord shared with them a number of valuable insights as to when they might expect to see His *parousia* and the end of the age. Matthew 24:27 contains what is probably one of the most significant elements of what Christ said about the events surrounding His *parousia:* "As the lightning comes forth from the east and flashes as far as the west, so will be the coming [*parousia*] of the Son of Man." That's hardly a secret event!

Our Lord also said the conditions that would characterize the time of His *parousia* would be like those that were prevalent in Noah's day. Then most of humankind "knew nothing" about the cataclysmic event about to take place "until the flood came and swept them all away." Jesus warned, "So too will be the coming [*parousia*] of the Son of Man" (Matthew 24:39). Notice that again, this was hardly a secret event!

Those who don't love God and His ways will consider the *parousia* of Christ to be a dreadful time, a time when their life will end. But for those who honor and love their Lord, the *parousia* will be a time of holy joy and of deliverance. John admonishes us: "Abide in him, so that when he is revealed we may have confidence and not be put to shame before him at his coming [*parousia*]" (1 John 2:28).

CHAPTER 13

Who Wrote the Book
of Hebrews?

The followers of Christ have treasured the New Testament book of Hebrews. Its chapters contain many answers to theological questions and numerous practical counsels pertaining to the daily life of the Christian. Consequently, Hebrews will continue to occupy a special position in the canon of New Testament writings.

But for some members of the faith, this book poses an important question: just who wrote it? The book never tells us who the author is. In this it differs significantly from the other letters of the New Testament. In all of them except the epistles of John, the name of the writer is the first word in the book.[1]

At one time most Christian theologians believed that the apostle Paul wrote the Epistle to the Hebrews—the ideas and reasoning of the epistle seem much like what one could expect to have come forth from his vigorous brain, and the content of this book is certainly in keeping with his understanding of Jewish religious teachings. But Hebrews

---

1. Second and Third John begin with the title of the author rather than his name; and First John doesn't directly identify its author.

doesn't say this, and there are reasons for considering that someone else wrote this book.

Some of those interested in this question have suggested that if Paul wasn't the author, the book must have been written by a close associate of his—someone who was well-versed in his way of thinking. People have proposed various individuals, such as Luke, Timothy, Apollos, Titus, and certain others who knew Paul's ideas. They suggest that this person valued Paul's teachings and wrote them down to save them for posterity.

There's no valid reason for rejecting Paul's authorship of Hebrews.

But since Hebrews doesn't identify its author, the challenge has remained— the question has continued to stimulate the imaginations and speculations of those in scholarly circles. Consequently, it has become increasingly commonplace for scholars to refer to the person who wrote this valuable letter simply as the "writer" or the "author" of the book of Hebrews, without mentioning any specific name.

One of the reasons scholars give for not attributing Hebrews to Paul is that the Greek vocabulary of the book differs from the vocabulary Paul used in the other letters he wrote. The idea is, of course, that if this letter is another Pauline epistle, it shouldn't differ so much from his other writings.

However, those who make this argument overlook an important factor: the Epistle to the Hebrews differs radically from all the other letters of Paul. In fact, it probably shouldn't be thought of nor labeled as a letter or epistle. Whoever wrote it simply has not given it the form of a personal letter. In contrast, all of the other written communications of the apostle Paul give evidence of being conversational letters addressed to specific persons or churches with whom he wished to commune in a very personal way, and they usually deal with specific personal and spiritual problems. On the other hand, the document that has been labeled "The Epistle to the Hebrews" doesn't have either the feel or the form of a personal communication. It simply is not a letter in the usual sense of the word.

The book of Hebrews gives much internal evidence of being nothing less than a collection of sermon notes that belonged to one of the early Christian evangelists—probably Paul. The format of the document's content varies considerably. In some places the statements are presented in carefully constructed literary detail, while at other times they have an abbreviated style in which some essential words have been omitted—perhaps with the intention that the speaker supply them as he preached from these notes.

The book begins with an elaborate, almost ponderous, statement that is so carefully worded that it can be favorably compared with some of the best productions of the Greek classical period. This eloquent opening statement seems to have been developed as an introduction meant to gain the attention of an educated or sophisticated audience. It is immediately followed by a short series of statements that seem somewhat less carefully crafted even though the thoughts stay on a rather high plane. The remainder of the book appears to have been devoted to various basic ideas and resource materials that the author wanted to consider while preaching the several sermon topics the book contains.

A survey of the book of Hebrews reveals the following:

- Quotations of a number of Old Testament texts, typically as found in the several Greek versions of the Old Testament.
- The introduction of these Old Testament texts by a suitable conjunction or prefatory remark; for example, "He says" (Hebrews 1:7); "And again, . . . he says" (Hebrews 1:6); "And again" (Hebrews 2:13); "Saying" (Hebrews 2:12); "And again in this place" (Hebrews 4:5); "When he said above" (Hebrews 10:8); etc.
- Frequent deductions, conclusions, and applications to be gained from a consideration of the Old Testament passages. Such practical applications are often introduced by "Therefore" (Greek: *dia touto*, Hebrews 2:1; or *dio*, Hebrews 3:7).
- The frequent use of the Greek postpositive conjunction *gar*, a conjunction that is typically translated "for." Elsewhere, this small word typically introduces a conclusion that can be deduced from the preceding statement. (For examples of its frequent appearance in the book of Hebrews, see Hebrews 7:1, 10, 11, 12, 13, 14, 17, 20, 26, 28.)
- The writer's use of the words *oun*, which has the general meaning of "therefore" (for example, see Hebrews 7:11; 8:4), and *hothen* (as in Hebrews 2:17; 3:1), when he isn't using the conjunction *gar*.

Most of those who challenge Pauline authorship of the book of Hebrews by appealing to the difference in vocabulary between it and Paul's epistles, his letters, ignore the implications of the five idiosyncrasies listed above. Hebrews appears to be notes from or for a series of evangelistic sermons and not an epistle, which would explain both the idiosyncrasies and the difference in vocabulary between it and Paul's epistles. So, there's no valid reason for rejecting Paul's authorship of this book.

CHAPTER 14

The Rest That Remains

Among the various sermon notes of Paul's that comprise the book of Hebrews (see chapter 13 of this book), one of the most complicated is the discourse on resting found in chapters 3 and 4. This lengthy passage presents a set of texts and propositions that aren't easy to follow—unless the reader takes pains to keep in mind the theme and purpose of this part of the book of Hebrews. One must remember that in this passage Paul was urging his readers— or more probably his audience, his hearers—*to be sure to enter God's rest.*

Paul begins by warning his hearers not to harden their hearts as Israel did during the forty years they wandered in the wilderness (Hebrews 3:7–9). Paul emphasizes the word *today* (verse 7), returning to it several times (see also Hebrews 3:13, 15; 4:7, 8). The way he develops this theme makes it evident that by "today," he means *any opportunity to accept God's gracious provision for our salvation.*

Paul then employs a number of symbolic illustrations of God's plan of salvation, some of which are quite concrete while others are almost hypothetical. But he always returns to the word *rest* as the ultimate symbol for entering a saving relationship with God.

In his initial illustration, Paul referred explicitly to the experience of Israel, speaking of God's original plan to lead that enslaved nation directly from Egypt into the homeland He had promised them in Canaan, where they certainly would have been able to rest. So, those early Christians who heard Paul speak may not have found it difficult to see a resemblance between the hope of the Israelites of old to enter physical Canaan and the Christians' hope of entering the land God has promised to believers.

Of course, the people of the Exodus rebelled, so, according to the book of Numbers (see chapter 14:33, 34), they weren't allowed to enter the rest God had in mind for them. In fact, Paul quotes God as saying about them, "In my anger I swore, 'They will not enter my rest' " (Hebrews 3:11). Instead, they had to wander around in the desert for forty long years—until nearly all the generation that had rebelled had died. It was only their children, then, who at the end of the forty years were finally allowed to enter the promised land of Canaan and the "rest" that was supposed to be theirs. Paul uses this initial illustration to urge his listeners not to make the same mistake and fail to take advantage of another "today"—that is, another day of opportunity to enter into rest (Hebrews 3:12–19).

As Paul continues his thoughts, he becomes increasingly explicit about applying this idea to our personal relationship to God (see Hebrews 4:1, 2). He says that when we hear the gospel preached, we, like the Israelites of old, receive an invitation to enter God's rest (verses 2, 3)—this *rest* apparently referring to freedom from the bondage of sin. Paul says we shouldn't even "seem" to come short of thus entering this wonderful spiritual rest (verse 1).

Then, in a surprising turn, Paul associates this spiritual rest with the rest provided by the seventh-day Sabbath, saying that God "spake in a certain place of the seventh day on this wise, And God did rest the seventh day from all his works" (Hebrews 4:4, KJV). Of course, when Paul makes this comparison with the seventh day, he is obviously building upon the idea of rest that is conveyed by the Hebrew word for *Sabbath*—which is a noun that is based upon a Hebrew verb that means "to rest."

The ancient Sabbath first appears all the way back in the story of Creation, which says that God blessed the seventh day of the week and made it holy because on it He rested from His work of creating (Genesis 2:2, 3). The seventh-day Sabbath was established to commemorate God's creative power. The fourth of the Ten Commandments continues that claim, explicitly saying that God made the Sabbath to commemorate the time when He created the world and everything in it (Exodus 20:11).

Paul and the other early Christians may have readily concluded that conversion to Christianity could be described as a new work of creation. Such a concept is, of course, to be found elsewhere in Paul's writings. For example, he wrote in 2 Corinthians 5:17, "If anyone is in Christ, he is a new creation" (NIV). Hence, if the Sabbath was originally a memorial of God's *creative* power, the early Christians could easily have regarded it also as a memorial of God's *redemptive* power—of the divine creative might that is miraculously manifested by the changed lives of Christian believers.

Such a possibility seems to have been foreshadowed in some of the Old Testament writings. For instance, the prophet Ezekiel pictures it as a symbol of character transformation. Ezekiel 20:12 says that God declares, "I gave them my sabbaths, to be a sign between me and them, that they might know that I am the LORD that sanctify them" (KJV). So it is obvious that by the time of the later Hebrew prophets, the Sabbath was becoming a symbol of God's recreative power—His power to change lives. Consequently, Paul, in his portrayal of God's desire for His people to enter His rest—first, that of the earthly Canaan, but ultimately, spiritual rest in Him—therefore pictures the Sabbath as symbolic of such a rest (Hebrews 4:4).

In Hebrews 4:6, Paul concludes that the Jews failed to fully enter God's rest. The evidence is that in the later Old Testament writings, God continued to offer His people "days"—opportunities—to enter the rest He had promised (verse 7). Paul states this explicitly, saying that David offered Israel a day of opportunity to enter that rest, which he wouldn't have done if Israel's entering the Promised Land under Joshua's[1] leadership had given them all that God had meant by the rest He had promised (verses 7, 8).

After speaking of Joshua's and then of David's later attempts to lead the Israelites into God's rest—and thus into the closer fellowship of spiritual rest with their Maker—and after speaking of the nature of a Sabbath rest as being representative of God's ultimate rest, Paul follows with one of the most amazing of New Testament thoughts. From the maze of interwoven ideas regarding rest, he concludes: "There remains, then, a Sabbath-rest for the people of God" (Hebrews 4:9, NIV).

---

1. The name *Jesus* in the King James Version of Hebrews 4:8 should read instead *Joshua*. *Jesus* is the Greek form of the Hebrew name *Joshua*—the name of the man who led Israel into Canaan, as the text says.

Very few modern translations present accurate renditions of the wording of this text in the Greek manuscripts. But the significance of the Greek text is clear; even a quick look at it leads one to realize that some decades after the Crucifixion, Paul believed that God was still calling people to experience Sabbath rest. In the next verse, Paul points out that this Sabbath rest is humankind's rest from their labors as God rested from His after He created the world and all that it contains. It is rest from our attempts to merit salvation by our own works—in faith, and also in obedience, resting in God for our deliverance, our salvation, which is both symbolized and made a reality as we keep the Sabbath.

The Greek word translated "Sabbath-rest" here is *sabbatismos,* a word that is made up of two parts: *sabbat,* a word that represents the original seventh-day Sabbath, and *-mos,* an action-noun ending. The word's meaning is clear even though many modern English translations tend to ignore it. Quite simply, it denotes the action or activity of keeping the Sabbath. And in the Greek Bible, the main verb in the sentence is *apoleipetai,* a form that is based on the verb *apoleipō,* which signifies that whatever it refers to is "left over," "left behind," "remains," or "continues on." So the verse says, as the New International Version translates it, "There remains, then, a Sabbath-rest for the people of God."

Thus the Sabbath—the seventh-day Sabbath of the commandments of God—continues to be a sign between God and His people, not only of His power to create the world of nature but also of His power to create new spiritual lives, changed lives—which, as we noted above, Ezekiel spoke of when he said the Sabbath was a sign of God's ability to sanctify His people, to make them holy. So, at a time when the world is becoming increasingly immersed in iniquity, when it needs more than ever to see lives changed by the creative power of its Maker, *a "Sabbath-rest"—Sabbath observance, a keeping of the Sabbath—still remains for the people of God.*

Note, then, that we have here a post-Crucifixion text that speaks directly to the question of whether or not early Christians had any place for a keeping of the seventh-day Sabbath. The answer is a clear-cut Yes.

Despite this, most present-day Christians have set apart Sunday in place of the seventh-day Sabbath, which they think of as the Jewish Sabbath. The reason they usually give for doing this is their desire to memorialize the day of Christ's resurrection.

Such a rationale, however, has a serious weakness that has usually been overlooked: the two days considered sacred by their proponents possess quite different characteristics. Though Sunday-keepers have a good intention, that of establishing a symbol of Christ's resurrection, they

SABBATISMOS:
Sabbath rest;
Sabbath observance

have set Sunday apart and treated it as sacred entirely on their own, human authority. In contrast, it was God Himself who established the seventh-day Sabbath.

Finding ways to celebrate what Christ's resurrection has done for us is certainly a praiseworthy thing, but the veneration of Sunday in honor of this important event doesn't fulfill the purpose for which God made a Sabbath of the seventh day of the week. A person may dislike the season of the year in which he was born and so celebrate his "birthday" on some other day of the year—but doing so doesn't change the actual date of his birth. In the same way, the human decision to establish a "sabbath" in honor of Christ's resurrection can never annul the weekly Sabbath God Himself gave us. Indeed, because of the rich symbolism conveyed by that day, Paul's statement still stands as a guide for God's people in these last days of this world: "There remains, then, a Sabbath-rest for the people of God."

CHAPTER 15

When It's Impossible
to Repent

A few years ago a young man came to his pastor deeply distressed and depressed. He was convinced that he was doomed, hopelessly lost, even though he longed to have a healthy Christian life. He was searching for a little assurance, hoping the pastor could give him some ray of light to lift the shadow that his concern had cast upon him.

His trouble? While searching the Bible to see what it says about repentance, he had come upon Hebrews 6:4–6 and was certain that those frightening verses applied to him. In the King James Version, which was the version he'd been reading, that passage says, "It is impossible for those who were once enlightened, and have tasted of the heavenly gift, and were made partakers of the Holy Ghost, and have tasted the good word of God and the powers of the world to come, if they shall fall away, to renew them again unto repentance; seeing they crucify to themselves the Son of God afresh and put him to an open shame."

The young man told the pastor that a short time back, he had accepted Christ as his Savior and had enjoyed an active Christian life. But he had allowed the temptations of the world to overwhelm his conversion and draw him off the Christian pathway. In short, he left his newfound experience and became a defeated, backslidden, former Christian.

Fortunately, he'd soon realized that his mistake of falling back into the world would result in a horrible loss, and he determined to find his way back to God—to repent and resume his walk with his Lord and enjoy a genuine spiritual life again. So, wanting to understand how to make his repentance as genuine and meaningful as possible, he'd been reading what the Bible had to say about it. That's what he was doing when he discovered the passage in Hebrews I've quoted above. It was clear and definite and seemed to point directly at him, so he concluded that he surely was eternally condemned and could never again have any hope for the future. His question was whether, in the light of this scripture, there was any reason to try again, any hope that God would accept him. The pastor responded, Yes, definitely!

We can't expect God's forgiveness while hanging on to an evil way of life.

How could he give that answer when the text seems so clear?

The answer lies in the fact that the version of the Bible that the young man was reading doesn't convey the meaning of the Greek text accurately. (The King James Version isn't the only one that's misleading here.) In order to know what these verses are really saying, we have to consider a small point of Greek grammar.

The critical point for this passage involves the parts of speech known as infinitives and participles. Briefly, these parts of speech are based on verbs but function like nouns. Infinitives combine the verb with the word *to*—"to see," "to go," etc. And, in their simplest English form, participles just add "-ing" to a verb—"seeing," "going," etc.

In Greek, infinitives and participles that have a present tense verbal stem depict a *continuing* activity, an *ongoing* activity. And participles with present tense verbal stems also typically indicate an action that is taking place simultaneously with another action. Hebrews 6:6 contains an infinitive ("to renew") and two participles, all of which have present tense verbal stems. Unfortunately, the King James Version and some modern translations ignore the impact these verbal stems should have on the translation of the verse—particularly, the meaning added by the two participles.

What Paul meant the passage to say becomes clear if these two participles are rendered in English by some such wording as "while _____-ing," or "as long as they are _____-ing," or by using some similar wording that makes it clear that the persons involved are continuing in sin, in rebellion. In the original Greek, the two key participles in this passage employ present tense verbal stems, so the action they describe is going on simultaneously with the action of the main verb. The grammar of Hebrews 6:4–6, then, tells us what Paul was saying about Christians who have returned in heart to their former lifestyle and orientation: "It is impossible . . . *to keep on* renewing [them] again and again unto repentance, *while* they are crucifying to themselves the Son of God afresh and *while* they are putting Him to open shame."

In other words, when Paul wrote this passage, he didn't intend it to discourage repentant people from seeking

God's forgiveness. No, he simply meant to warn them against thinking they can have life both ways. As long as people prefer to continue in their old way of life, their worldly habits and sinful practices, they can't expect to receive acceptance and forgiveness from God. On the other hand, people who sincerely want to find God's acceptance and forgiveness and who want to quit sinning will find a loving heavenly Father who is more than willing to welcome them back and to freely forgive their past waywardness. So, Hebrews 6:4–6 doesn't in any way contradict the encouraging promise of 1 John 1:9: "If we confess our sins, he who is faithful and just will forgive us our sins and cleanse us from all unrighteousness."

Thus, the pastor was able to tell the worried young man that the passage in Hebrews wasn't meant to discourage him nor any other repentant sinner from coming back to God. He told him that the passage simply warns us against thinking that we can expect God's approval while hanging on to an evil way of life. On the other hand, any sincere hunger we have for God's forgiveness and acceptance is in itself evidence that God's Holy Spirit is at work in our lives, drawing us to our heavenly Father, who offers us the forgiveness we crave.

CHAPTER 16

Melchizedek:
Forerunner of Jesus

The book of Hebrews introduces us to Melchizedek, but its few brief descriptions of this man leave us wondering about the personage behind the name. Nevertheless, Melchizedek must have been an important man, because Paul says that Jesus was "made an high priest for ever after the order of Melchisedec" (Hebrews 6:20, KJV).

Scripture doesn't yield much personal information about this mystery man. He first appears in Genesis 14:18–20; David mentions him in Psalm 110:4; and Paul writes about him in Hebrews 5:6, 10; 6:20; 7:1–24. From these few scriptural passages the following details emerge.

- He was the "king of Salem" (later called Jerusalem), a title that Paul explains means "king of peace" (Genesis 14:18; Hebrews 7:2).
- His personal name, Melchizedek, means "king of righteousness" (Hebrews 7:2; the name is spelled in several different ways in the various translations).
- "He was the priest of the most high God" (Genesis

14:18, KJV; cf. Hebrews 7:1).
- He was "without father, without mother, without genealogy, having neither beginning of days nor end of life" (Hebrews 7:3)—probably just a convenient way of saying that neither his history nor his genealogy were preserved in the sacred writings.
- He is described as "resembling the Son of God" in that "he remains a priest forever" (Hebrews 7:3).
- Paul reverses the perspective, comparing Jesus to Melchizedek in that Jesus became "a high priest forever according to the order of Melchizedek" (Hebrews 6:20).

With only these few details to guide us, we may well ponder such questions as the identity of this great king who was also a priest, how he could have been brought into existence without parents, and why Jesus' priesthood had to be "according to the order of Melchizedek." However, while what the Bible tells us about the ancient king Melchizedek awakens our curiosity, even intense searching yields few facts, so for the most part, this character will have to remain one of the great unsolved mysteries of the Bible. Yet the facts we do have make some important points.

In the first place, Paul obviously wished to speak of Jesus as a wonderfully gracious High Priest—One who is beautifully patient with all our human weaknesses because He "was in all points tempted like as we are, yet without sin" (Hebrews 4:15, KJV). But how could Jesus of Nazareth be a high priest—or a simple, ordinary priest for that matter—when He didn't belong to a priestly family? All Jewish people knew full well that only descendants of Aaron, of the tribe of Levi, could serve as priests, and Jesus had been born into the royal family of David, which came from the tribe of Judah and not even from the tribe of Levi, to say nothing of the family of Aaron. So, as far as the Jews were concerned, Jesus' genealogy disqualified Him for the priesthood.

Consequently, Jesus' genealogy posed a problem for Paul and others who wished to explain His nature and ministry. How could His serving in the high-priestly office be explained in a way that would satisfy those who would be concerned about His genealogical qualifications? It appears that the writer of the book of Hebrews looked for some other priesthood besides the Aaronic priesthood and providentially found this need met in the priesthood of the godly king of the ancient Canaanite city of Salem.

If Melchizedek could be a priest, so could Jesus.

Two parts of the Old Testament, Genesis 14 and Psalm 110:4, describe this mysterious man as a valid high priest, one who ministered in the name of the true God even though he was also the king of a heathen city. Neither of these scriptures links him to the family of Aaron or the tribe of Levi. In fact, Melchizedek, the priest-king of Salem, lived long before either Aaron or even Aaron's forefather, Levi, was born. Hence Paul could point to Melchizedek as evidence that there was precedent to Christ's functioning as a priest despite a genealogy that didn't include Aaron. Such a priestly order was all the more appropriate in view of several important factors:

- As Genesis 14 makes clear, Melchizedek's credentials

were so well respected that the patriarch Abraham gave both tithe and honor to him.

- Because in a sense Abraham carried the chromosomes and genes of both the tribe of Levi and the family of Aaron in his body when he paid tithe to the priest-king of Salem, it could be said that even *they* recognized the superiority of his office and mediation.
- Apparently, Paul believed that Psalm 110 is a prophecy of the Messiah (see verse 1), and he quotes verse 4 as offering support for the legitimacy of Christ's functioning as a priest: "The Lord hath sworn, and will not repent, Thou art a priest for ever after the order of Melchizedek" (KJV).
- The fact that, like the original story in Genesis 14, the Messianic prophecy of Psalm 110 doesn't add any details regarding the genealogy of the Messiah to come makes this application even more plausible— because, of course, Christ existed without parents during the uncounted ages before He appeared on earth as our Redeemer.

Therefore, the author of the book of Hebrews had no problem with identifying Christ as our great High Priest even though He was clearly not a member of the priestly family of Aaron. (See also the logical summary in Hebrews 7:4–17, 25–28.) According to him, Jesus had the right to function as High Priest because He belonged to the priesthood of Melchizedek, and the mysteries surrounding *that* order of priests were sufficient to obviate any criticism of that conclusion.

Discussion closed.

CHAPTER 17

Salvation: Contract, Will, or Both?

It seems that the writers of the New Testament occasionally threw in a beautiful pun or some other play on words to catch the imagination of their readers. The apostle Paul seems to have enjoyed words that have more than one meaning, and his wordplay is particularly interesting because he was skilled enough to use these words in such a way that both their meanings communicate truths!

An interesting example of such artistry shows up in Paul's employment of the Greek word *diathēkē,* an ancient term that possessed two rather common but different meanings. On one hand, *diathēkē* denoted a contract—an agreement between two or more parties, affirmed by witnesses, that bound the parties to the terms they had agreed upon. When the parties to the contract were national governments, the resulting document would be what we call a treaty. In English usage in the past, such agreements—whether treaties or contracts—were often called *covenants,* so the Greek word *diathēkē* is frequently translated in English Bibles as "covenant."

But a *diathēkē* could also be a will. A will has at least

three characteristics: (1) It isn't an agreement between two or more parties but the expression of the desires, the will, of one party. (2) Its terms can be carried out only after the death of the person who made it. (3) And its terms can't be changed once the person who made it has died.

Since the word *diathēkē* has at least two meanings, "contract" and "will," translating it can be confusing. Usually, though, the context of the word makes clear which meaning is intended. Does the writer mean an agreement between two or more parties or about a document that contains terms that can be enforced only after someone's death? However, in at least one place, Paul mingled the two concepts together, taking advantage of the double meaning of the term.

DIATHĒKĒ:

contract; covenant;

last will and testament

In Hebrews chapters 7 through 10, the apostle dwells at length upon the *diathēkē* that God has established between Himself and His people. (Note especially Hebrews 7:22; 8:6–13; 9:1, 16, 17; and 10:15–23.) To fully understand his use of *diathēkē,* we need to sort out and clarify several aspects of his discussion. First, let's note that he's obviously writing about *two* covenants or agreements. He refers to one of them as the "first" covenant (e.g., Hebrews 9:1), and the second he calls "a new covenant" (Hebrews 8:13).

It's clear that what Paul calls the "first covenant" involved the provisions of the Mosaic law and "ordinances of divine service, and a worldly sanctuary" (Hebrews 9:1, KJV). This particular covenant—or "agreement," or even "contract"—appears to have been made on the basis of the Israelites' agreement to serve God. ("All the people answered together, and said, All that the LORD hath spoken we will do," Exodus 19:8, KJV; see also 19:5.) But Paul says there's a second covenant—the "new covenant"—which he always depicts as being based upon what *God* will do for His people. For example, Hebrews 10:16, 17 describes this covenant in these words: "This is the covenant that I will make with them after those days, saith the Lord, I will put my laws into their hearts, and in their minds will I write them; and their sins and iniquities will I remember no more" (KJV; see also Hebrews 8:7–13).

As Paul expands the ideas that distinguish these two covenants (or contracts), he interjects a rather novel thought, one that's difficult to render clearly in English because no single English word does what the Greek term *diathēkē* does—none of our words means both "contract" and "will." The subtle added thought is especially expressed in the Greek wording of Hebrews 9:16, 17, which we can legitimately translate as saying, "Where there is a *diathēkē,* the death of the one who made it must occur, because a *diathēkē* is valid [only] at death, since it is not in force when the one who made it [still] lives."

The apostle introduces this particular aspect of the *diathēkē* in Hebrews 9:12–15 by drawing a contrast between the ratifications of the two covenants (see verses 18ff). He points out that the first covenant involved the blood of animals, but the blood active in the "new covenant" is the blood of Christ. This covenant—or will—was put into force by the death of Christ, the One who made it (see verse 17). And Christ's death was obviously far more important and effective than the death of animals.

Thus Paul splices together at least two great themes. He wants us to understand clearly that the new plan of God— the "new covenant," the new *diathēkē*—involves a transaction between God and the human heart (in other words, our minds) in which by the power of His Spirit, He makes it possible for us to obey Him. And this covenant—which He has made without asking for our input—*has been ratified by the death of His Son.* So this covenant, which is also a will, can never be nullified because the One who "wrote" it has died.

People who read this passage in English may find it difficult to follow the apostle's discussion because it involves a subtle play on words—a double meaning that cannot be expressed in English by a single word. However, when we recognize what the apostle was saying and how he was saying it, we can discern his meaning and take new courage in God's plan for us.

CHAPTER 18

Just Exactly What Is God's Glory?

Glory is one of those words that we tend to feel we understand pretty well. However, if we were to be asked to give a quick definition of the word, we might hesitate a bit and then have to admit that we couldn't define it off the top of our head—at least not without a little time to think it over. Given that time, we might eventually say that it means something very bright and shiny, or that it signifies something like *praise,* or that we relate this word to *fame* and *honor.*

DOXA:

glory; splendor; honor—a good and merciful character

What does the word *glory* really mean? More specifically, what did the New Testament writers have in mind when they wrote of *doxa,* the Greek term that's translated "glory" in English versions of the Bible?

To begin with, the Greek word means "brightness," "brilliance," "splendor." But we must also note that most of the men who wrote the New Testament were well acquainted with a Semitic word, the Hebrew version of which was *kabod*. The root meaning of this term is "weight," and it had connotations something like the English idiom "he threw his weight around." In other words, the Hebrew term *kabod* had connotations of strength and solidity. These then morphed into the extended connotations of *value* and *reputation* and *influence*—of qualities that attract people's attention and admiration.

Christian writers of the first century used the classical Greek word *doxa*. However, they didn't restrict their use of it to the ways that the non-Christian writers of that time employed the word. The Christian writers added new trails of meaning for *doxa,* bestowing many of the Hebrew concepts connected with *kabod* on this Greek word. Because they did, when we read the word "glory" in the New Testament, we have to think of it in terms of *kabod*. The meaning of the Hebrew term should help us to understand better just what the writers of the New Testament meant. So, let's consider the various nuances of *doxa*.

First, the New Testament writers used the term to describe the brilliance they saw surrounding heavenly beings. For example, the word seems to have this meaning in Luke 9:32, where Luke uses it to describe the appearance of Christ and His two visitors on the Mount of Transfiguration (cf. also verse 29). Similarly, we may see the idea of brilliance in the description of the angels who sang for the shepherds when Christ was born (see Luke 2:9); we're told the shepherds "were terrified" when they saw the "glory of the Lord" with which the angel—or perhaps the whole angelic choir—came. And when, to illustrate a point he was making, the apostle Paul wrote, "There is one glory of the sun, and another glory of the moon, and another glory of the stars; indeed, star differs from star in glory" (1 Corinthians 15:41), he was doubtless thinking of the different degrees of brilliance these heavenly bodies have.

Second, New Testament passages frequently employ the term "glory" (*doxa*) to refer to the quality in a person that awakens admiration in others, thus echoing one of the primary meanings of the Hebrew *kabod*. Related to this concept is the feeling of pride in one's own attributes. Jesus rejected this feeling, telling His opponents, "I do not seek my own glory" (John 8:50).

Third, given the general meaning of "glory" in the New Testament, the expression has become a synonym of the words *praise* and *honor* as found in some of Scripture's songs of praise. Examples of this usage are easily found (see, e.g., Luke 2:14; Romans 11:36; etc).

A final thought that may be significant here: when we link the New Testament concept with the Hebrew word *kabod,* we should consider the experience that Moses had involving this word. On one occasion when he met God on Mount Sinai, he blurted out, "Show me your glory, I pray" (Exodus 33:18). God's response to his request indicates that Moses wanted to know which of God's attributes God felt most aroused people's admiration. God's reply should give us all great joy because it revealed that He regards His great glory as being His grace and mercy toward the undeserving. Shortly after Moses made his request, he gave God the two stone tablets on which God would write the Ten Commandments. Then, Scripture says, "The LORD passed before him, and proclaimed, 'The LORD, the LORD, a God merciful and gracious, slow to anger, and abounding in steadfast love and faithfulness, keeping steadfast love for the thousandth generation, forgiving iniquity and transgression and sin' " (Exodus 34:6, 7).

The fact that God Himself takes pleasure in His own grace and patience and views this as His personal *kabod* is a wonderful bit of news for all of us. Apparently, this was His special glory in the times of both the Old and New Testaments. It is still His attitude toward me and toward you and toward all undeserving but needy human beings.

CHAPTER 19

Is Christ Merely *a* God?

In a context that calls Jesus "the Word," the great embodiment of God's communication to humankind, He is also called *theos,* "God": "In the beginning . . . the Word was God [*theos*]" (John 1:1). But the definite article (Greek, *ho;* "the") that those who read Greek might expect to see with *theos* ("God") isn't there, and since nouns that don't have the definite article often are meant to be understood as indefinite, some people—among them, Jehovah's Witnesses—have come to believe that Christ is God only in the sense that He is *a* God, which could also mean that He is subordinate to—isn't equal to—the eternal Father, *the* God. Just what was John saying when he wrote *"theos ēn ho logos"*—"the Word was God"? How does leaving out the definite article affect the meaning of this clause?

Our belief that God inspired all of Scripture means that our interpretation of this important passage must not in any way contradict the teachings of the rest of Scripture, and Scripture clearly and unreservedly speaks of Jesus Christ as being fully divine. For instance, the apostle Paul wrote, "In him the whole fullness of deity dwells bodily"

(Colossians 2:9). In fact, a sizeable number of other New Testament passages very clearly refer to Christ as *theos,* "God," *and have the definite article right where we would expect to see it.* Hebrews 1:8, for example, has the articular *theos,* and it is obviously speaking of Christ: "Of the Son he [God the Father] says, 'Your throne, O God [*ho theos*], is forever and ever.' " The *ho* that precedes *theos* is the Greek definite article.

Hebrews 1:8: "Of the Son he [God the Father] says, 'Your throne, O God [ho theos], is forever and ever.' "

Acts 20:28 contains the phrase *tēn ekklēsian tou theou,* "the church of God." In this phrase, the words "of God" came from the Greek *tou theou,* which translated more literally would read "of *the* God" (emphasis added). Again, the Greek wording has the definite article before *theou,* the word that means "God." Notice that Paul immediately expands the thought with a helpful explanation: "the church of God that he obtained *with his own blood*" (margin; emphasis added). This explanation makes it obvious that the God referred to in this sentence is the One who purchased the church "with his own blood"—clearly a reference to Christ.

One more example: when Thomas acknowledged the resurrected Christ, he exclaimed, "My Lord and my God!" (John 20:28). In the Greek original, that reads, *"Ho kurios mou kai ho theos mou!"* Note that we have here another instance of a reference to Christ as God in which the article *ho* precedes the word *theos,* "God."

Sometimes, Jehovah's Witnesses claim that Scripture

distinguishes between God the Father, "the mighty God," and Jesus, the Son of God. But Scripture doesn't support even this distinction. In his prophetic picture of the Messiah to come, Isaiah says, "His name shall be called . . . The mighty God" (Isaiah 9:6, KJV).

So, while *anarthrous* Greek nouns (nouns without an article) can be the equivalent of indefinite nouns in English (nouns preceded by *a* or *an*), they are so *only* if both the context and the way the noun is used in the rest of Scripture point to its being indefinite. And as we have seen from the various examples presented, Scripture doesn't picture Jesus as merely *a* God—a lower-ranking deity than the Father. No, it presents Jesus as fully divine—just as divine, just as fully God, as the Father is.

If in John 1:1, *theos* without the article doesn't mean "a God," what *does* it mean? What idea *did* John intend to communicate in this verse?

Besides using *anarthrous* nouns as indefinite nouns, the Bible writers also used them *to express the quality or nature of an accompanying noun.* We can see the force of this usage in 1 John 4:8: "Whoever does not love does not know God, for God is love." In this statement, "love" is *anarthrous,* but that doesn't mean John was trying to say that God is "*a* love"—love of indefinite content and quality. Rather, the *anarthrous* construction here obviously means that love describes the very *nature* of God, and the clause could justifiably be translated "the nature of God is love" or even "the essence of God is love."

This usage suggests that in the first verse of his Gospel, John wasn't saying that Jesus, the Word, was "a god"—one god among a number of gods. Rather, he was saying that the Word was by nature God/Deity/divine. In fact, in verse

14 of this chapter John describes Him further in this way: "*The Word* became flesh and lived among us, and we have seen his glory, the glory as of the Father's only Son, full of grace and truth" (margin; emphasis added).

This Word demands our attention. We need to listen to Him, to learn from Him, to obey Him, to worship Him.

CHAPTER 20

Even God Needs Patience

An interesting—even fascinating—side of God's character and personality is hinted at in a verse that is tucked away and almost hidden among the messages to the seven churches. In the New Revised Standard Version, the promise to the church of Philadelphia reads: "Because you have kept my word of patient endurance, I will keep you from the hour of trial that is coming on the whole world to test the inhabitants of the earth" (Revelation 3:10). In this rendering, the critical wording is "my word of patient endurance," a phrase that could also be translated "the word of my patience," as the King James Version gives it.

The term *word* in this verse is translated from the Greek word *logos*—which can also mean "matter" or "concern" (see, e.g., Acts 8:21). So the thought presented here may well be that there's a matter or concern that constantly occupies

HUPOMONĒ:

remain under something;

bear with patience or

patient endurance

our heavenly Parent. We're so concerned with our own day-to-day worries that we seldom stop to think that our great heavenly Father may also have to deal with an ongoing concern. We probably should occasionally ponder just how *we* might feel if we had created a race of beings who turned out to be as selfish and obstinately rebellious as we have. Would we have been able to temper our feelings and wait year after year—and even century after long century— in the hope of seeing some of the race be *somewhat* loyal to their creator?

The point is that *God has had to be patient*! Don't you imagine that the centuries of repeated disappointments He's had to endure must have challenged His patience at times? The Greek word of interest in the phrase we've focused on in this chapter is *hupomonē,* a term that literally means to "remain under" something, to bear something with patience, or patient endurance. In Revelation 3:10, God commends the members of the church of Philadelphia for being concerned about Him because of the patience His rebellious sons and daughters have made necessary on His part. He adds that He will reward the Philadelphians well for their interest in *His* matter.

Actually, there's a profound reason why our heavenly Father is willing to be patient. He is committed to giving all the descendants of Adam and Eve a full opportunity to become loyal to His government if they wish to do so. God won't bring things on earth to an end until every person has come face-to-face with this great opportunity and made his or her decision clear. Second Peter 3:9 makes this point directly: "The Lord is not slow about his promise, as some think of slowness, but is patient with you, not wanting any to perish, but all to come to repentance."

So God treats each of us with patience—for which we should feel eternally thankful! Apparently, He's pleased when He finds some of us also feeling a bit sympathetic toward *Him* for the heavy load that *He's* been carrying these many years—these many wearisome centuries! He has pronounced a special blessing upon those who empathize with Him. Don't overlook it!

CHAPTER 21

One of Satan's Slippery Slopes

The disciple Peter—who had been a fisherman, and thus a man of the sea—certainly was a dramatic character who rather naturally draws our attention whenever we consider the sad events of the Passion Week. We see him particularly as the person who, to save his own skin during those emotion-filled days, pitifully yielded to the temptation to deny his Lord.

Some people who tell Peter's shameful story point to the scriptural statement that he supported the truthfulness of his denials with cursing and swearing (Matthew 26:74). Often, they picture Peter's actions and words in ways that Scripture doesn't support.

The whole story is so dramatic and yet so instructive that we may find it both quite interesting and quite helpful to explore some of the painful details. We certainly will pose the question of just what kind of language Peter used that night as he desperately tried to prove that he had absolutely no relationship to the accused Prisoner.

Some of those who analyze this story almost seem to enjoy picturing Peter as a crude man of the sea who by

nature and occupation was inclined to burst into blasphe-
mies and foul language in order to support his assertions. I
remember hearing a preacher say, "And you know how
sailors are!" implying, of course, that seafaring men are
known for their "salty" speech—for punctuating their statements with uncouth and irreverent language. However,
analyses of Peter's experience that accept such assumptions
completely miss what really happened when he denied being someone who followed Jesus.

The wording of the first question that Peter was asked
sheds an interesting light on the story. The young woman
who asked this question, a doorkeeper, phrased her query
in such a way as *to make No the only appropriate answer*. In
effect, this woman very diplomatically said, "You certainly
are *not* one of this Man's disciples, are you?" Thus she en-
abled the disciple to reply with a shrug of his shoulders,
"No, I'm not," and then to continue making his way into
the courtyard of the high priest's house. Peter probably
didn't have to give much thought to the first denial. The
tempter made it so natural, so easy, for the words to slip
out of his mouth.

The original Greek wording of the second temptation
Peter faced also encouraged him to deny being a follower
of Jesus. The questioner says, "You are surely *not* also one
of His disciples, are you?" The question was posed and
phrased so nicely that to be cordial in return, the tempted
disciple almost *had* to agree with his tempter—so Peter replied again, with no apparent hesitation, "No, I'm not."

The first and second denials were slippery slopes that
were almost invisible—slopes on which the unsuspecting
disciple began to slide toward spiritual disaster. He had
turned against his Lord almost without realizing what he

was doing. But in the third temptation, the devil employed a more vicious strategy. This time the question was neither courteous nor diplomatic. Satan turned on Peter the heat of apparent danger and then presented the temptation in clear, positive terms: "One of the servants of the high priest, a relative of him whose ear Peter cut off, said, 'Did I not see you in the garden with Him'?" (John 18:26).

"You know how sailors are!"

This time the wording of the question calls for the answer Yes. But Peter knew that the one who asked the question was most likely hostile, and that if he answered Yes, he might be arrested as Jesus was, and he no doubt feared what that might lead to. This is where the curses and swearing come into the story.

However, though Peter resorted to curses and swearing, he didn't use foul and blasphemous language in an attempt to convince his interrogators that he was too crude and ir-religious a person to have associated with Jesus. Rather, he "swore" a solemn oath and called fearful curses down upon himself to convince those who questioned him that he was telling the truth (see Matthew 26:74). In swearing an oath, people would raise their right hand and call upon God or heaven or some holy person or place to be as a supernatural witness to the truthfulness of some statement that was in question. (Compare Matthew 5:33–37, where Christ advised His followers not to swear such oaths.) In using "curses," people would invite God to bring some drastic punishment upon them if what they were saying wasn't true—in essence, this was a kind of prayer. Children do something similar when they say things like, "It was Jimmy! Really! Cross my heart and hope to die!"

In Peter's day, it was commonly believed that few people would lie while swearing an oath or asking God to curse them if they were lying. So being confronted by someone who recognized him must have so terrified Peter that he felt he must take those extreme measures to convince people that he was telling the truth when he denied being a follower of Jesus—something much worse than foul language ever has been. Of course, it was then that he heard a rooster crowing somewhere nearby.

The story of Peter's denials contains an interesting if not particularly significant detail. In Matthew 26:73, one of Peter's questioners says Peter's speech gives him away. In this case, the questioner means that Peter sounds more like a native of Galilee than someone from Judea (see Mark 14:70; Luke 22:59).

The records we have of those days suggest that the people of Galilee were more well-spoken than were those from Judea, and especially citizens of Jerusalem. So even though Peter was originally a seaman, he probably shouldn't be characterized as a man whose speech was rough and uncouth. Instead, he probably was well-spoken—his speech simply betraying him as a Galilean, as was Jesus.

More important, Peter's experience warns us that giving in to "small" temptations prepares us to yield to larger ones—to temptations that now we may think we'd never succumb to.

CHAPTER 22

How to Have *Exuberant Joy*!

It may seem that Scripture encourages us to maintain a rather serious attitude. After all, we're engaged in a continuing war, and we must not only struggle for victory over temptations and sin in our own lives, but we're also supposed to be engaged in life-and-death struggles to rescue others from the powers of evil. This situation has tended to make Christians adopt a sober outlook.

However, Scripture also openly encourages us to experience a sense of joy and happiness. In fact, a number of passages rather clearly promote such an attitude. Exclamations such as the following are sprinkled throughout God's Word.

- "I have trusted in your steadfast love; my heart shall *rejoice* in your salvation" (Psalm 13:5; emphasis added).
- "Let the righteous be *joyful;* let them *exult* before God; let them *be jubilant with joy*" (Psalm 68:3; emphasis added).
- "This is the day that the LORD has made; let us *re-*

joice and *be glad* in it" (Psalm 118:24; emphasis added).

And the New Testament pictures Jesus as urging or even commanding us to rejoice.

- "*Rejoice* that your names are written in heaven" (Luke 10:20; emphasis added).
- "You heard me say to you, 'I am going away, and I am coming to you.' *If you loved me, you would rejoice* that I am going to the Father, because the Father is greater than I" (John 14:28; emphasis added).

In fact, Jesus commands His people to find a reason for expressing joy even during times of stress and persecution: "Blessed are you when people revile you and persecute you and utter all kinds of evil against you falsely on my account. *Rejoice* and *be glad,* for your reward is great in heaven, for in the same way they persecuted the prophets who were before you" (Matthew 5:11, 12; emphasis added).

Proof that the Bible isn't opposed to joy can also be seen in the fact that the New Testament contains half a dozen Greek words meaning "joy," "rejoicing," and so forth—an impressive treasury of words that encourage the followers of Christ to be happy. (The Old Testament has at least twelve different Hebrew words related to these emotions!)

Among the New Testament passages that encourage attitudes of joy, there are two verses that employ a most interesting—if unusual—expression. They read: "We have gifts that differ according to the grace given to us: . . . the exhorter, in exhortation; the giver, in generosity; the leader, in diligence; the compassionate, in *cheerfulness*" (Romans

12:6–8; emphasis added). "Each of you must give as you have made up your mind, not reluctantly or under compulsion, for God loves a *cheerful* giver" (2 Corinthians 9:7; emphasis added).

The Greek adjective translated "cheerful" is *hilaros,* a word that can also mean "happy" and "joyous." Paul wants us to be happy when we contribute to our fellow believers who are in need. In Romans 12:8, he instructs us to perform our acts of mercy with "cheerfulness." Here, the apostle employed the related Greek noun *hilarotēs,* a word that generally denotes an attitude of happiness.

What makes these Greek expressions especially interesting is that they are built on the ancient Greek root *hilar-,* which English speakers borrowed to create the English noun *hilarity.* This English word has been stretched beyond the meaning of the original Greek root, reaching past cheerfulness and joy to denote something that is extremely funny or that is marked by or causes hilarity, which, in turn, is defined as "noisy merriment; boisterous gaiety."[1]

HILAROS:

cheerful; glad; merry

Even though the New Testament terms *hilaros* and *hilarotēs* didn't possess the almost frivolous significance of their modern derivatives, they may already have been moving in that direction, having by that time come to mean something like "exuberant joy." If so, it is certainly interesting and significant that terms such as these should show up in the New Testament descriptions of how we should feel when we perform kind

---

1. *Webster's New World Dictionary* (Cleveland and New York: Simon & Schuster, 1988), s.v. "Hilarity."

deeds for our fellow human beings. Surely, it wouldn't be bad for us to feel enthusiastic joy on such occasions. A little bit of the New Testament brand of hilarity might actually even enable us to sleep better at night—especially when we remember that God loves a *hilarious* giver!

CHAPTER 23

Did God Change His Mind?

The supernatural vision must have been extremely troubling to the apostle Peter. For one thing, what he saw was strange—even bizarre. And what he was told to do was something that he considered wrong, sinful even—something that he absolutely would never have thought of doing. It seemed that he was being told to eat things that were *unclean* and totally *unfit* for food. Even the thought of it was revolting!

It had all happened so suddenly. The Bible tells us that it occurred around noon (Acts 10:9). While the apostle was waiting for his friends to prepare the midday meal, he had gone upstairs onto the flat roof to be alone while he engaged in a time of personal devotions. Then his reflective moments were interrupted by this heaven-sent vision—one that was startling in the challenge it brought to his beliefs.

In the vision, Peter saw a large sheet that held numerous animals—"all kinds of four-footed creatures and reptiles and birds" (verse 12)—that was being lowered to the ground in front of him. The Jews considered the reptiles unclean, spiritually contaminating—and perhaps some of the quadrupeds and birds in the sheet were of unclean species as well.[1] According to the Jewish teachings of that day, clean animals and clean human beings could be defiled by mingling with or even just touching unclean people or animals, and those who were defiled were considered unfit to participate in religious services until they were cleansed. Such people and animals were thought to have become ceremonially "common" (Acts 10:14, KJV) or "profane" (NRSV). In fact, it was rather freely taught that people might even become unclean if they entered the house of a Gentile or allowed a Gentile to enter their house. The religious customs of that day called for the utter separation of Jews and Gentiles.

In the vision, Peter was commanded, "Get up, Peter; kill and eat" (verse 13). No doubt baffled by this command, the apostle remonstrated, "By no means, Lord," he said, "for I have never eaten anything that is profane or unclean" (verse 14). The voice responded, "What God has made clean, you must not call profane" (verse 15). The command was given two more times, similar responses followed, and then the sheet was snatched up to heaven.

While Peter was wondering what this vision could possibly mean, he heard somebody at the front gate, asking whether he was staying there. The Spirit of God told him that some Gentile men had come to invite him to go with them to their master's house and there instruct him in the truths of his God and the risen Christ. Peter connected the dots and realized that God was inaugurating a completely new view of Gentiles. The vision meant that associating

---

1. God had given Moses the basic principles (see Leviticus 11; Deuteronomy 14; and, e.g., Leviticus 20:24–26).

with the Gentiles wouldn't defile Christians. Peter and his fellow Christians were no longer to shun the Gentiles; in fact, they were to share the good news of the gospel freely with them.

No doubt as Peter accompanied the Gentile messengers, he felt deeply conflicted because of the challenge to beliefs and practices that were almost part of his being; but he *did* go, and he *did* enter the home of the Gentile family. Once inside, he recounted the peculiar vision and explained what was troubling him. And since Peter now understood the point of the vision, he freely shared the gospel with the Gentile household.

Some have thought this vision of Peter's might have been God's way of informing us that the animals once considered unclean He has now declared to be clean and therefore fit to be eaten. But in a helpful article, Colin House points out that Peter "was never directed to consume the 'unclean' creature, but rather immediately to desist from describing as 'common' the creatures that God had declared *'cleansed.'*" [2]

A close reading of this story reveals that it wasn't meant to deal with the question of what foods Christians may eat. Rather, it's the story of a vivid method that God used to inform a rigid disciple that he should be willing to associate with Gentiles and to share with them the good news of the gospel. In the context of missionary work, Gentiles are now neither unclean nor "common," and Peter and the other believers could now freely preach to them.

Obviously, this was good news for both the Gentiles

---

2. Colin House, "Defilement by Association: Some Insights From the Usage of KOINOS/KOINOŌ in Acts 10 and 11," *Andrews University Seminary Studies* 21, no. 2 (1983): 148.

and the Jews. In fact, as the life of the church unfolded thereafter, the greater part of those who accepted the Christian message were Gentiles. We take this fact so much for granted that it now seems rather strange that at one time, Jewish Christians—both laity and leaders—wondered whether they should even try to share the gospel with Gentiles—that they believed that such a close relationship with Gentiles might seriously contaminate their relationship with God.

"What God has made clean, you must not call profane."

The facts laid out above make apparent to us what the purpose of the strange vision was. It had nothing to do with "clean" and "unclean" foods as such, but rather was written to clarify for early Christians the fact that whatever "cleanness" they possessed wouldn't suffer defilement (i.e., render them "common") because of the contacts they had with the Gentiles in their work of sharing the good news of the gospel. Consequently, Peter and his fellow apostles immediately took up the vocation, working with great energy to evangelize the numerous Gentile communities of the Mediterranean world and beyond—a mission that has continued unabated to the present day, when the greatest portion of the world's Christian population that is made up of "Gentile" believers far exceeds the portion made up of Jewish converts. This is the fruitage of Peter's strange vision of so long ago and far away.

CHAPTER 24

The Essential Faith

What is *faith*? As Christians, we use this word so often that there's a distinct danger that we'll forget what it means. Whatever faith is, it must be important, because Scripture says that we can't please God if we don't have it (see Hebrews 11:6). In view of this, the followers of Christ do well to make sure they understand the significance and meaning of faith.

Pistis, the New Testament Greek term that's translated "faith," is a member of a sizeable family of related words. As such, it bears some of the nuances of a number of its verbal relatives. For example, the verb *pisteuō*—a word that is typically translated "to believe"—is a major member of this larger family of words. Hence the related (and derived) noun *faith* doubtless bears much of the idea of "belief." But faith isn't equivalent to *belief* alone; *belief* doesn't tell us all that *faith* means. James 2:19 makes this clear when it says that "even the demons believe—and shudder." Obviously, then, belief alone doesn't make us right with God or guarantee us salvation.

Another significant member of the same word family is

the adjective *pistos,* a term that characterizes a person as "faithful" or "trustworthy." This adjective likely arose from the idea that one could *believe* that the people said to have this characteristic would *act* in the way they were supposed to. They could be trusted.

So, while the New Testament term translated "faith" certainly rests on the foundation of belief, it also appears to include the thought of reliance upon the trustworthiness of the person or thing in which we place our belief, our faith. Thus the idea of trust probably forms a large part of the biblical concept of faith. Notice, for instance, that when, in Hebrews 11:6, Paul speaks of the importance of this virtue and declares that we cannot please God without it, he adds the explanation that it is essential for those who approach God to "believe that he exists and that he rewards those who seek him." We must place our *trust* (our *faith*) in the One who is eminently worthy of our trust.

PISTEUŌ:
to believe

Another facet of *pistis,* the Greek term translated "faith," is revealed by the way it's spelled. In Greek, words that end in *–is* are nouns of action. Many of the Greek nouns that have this ending are nouns that portray mental rather than physical activity—for instance, *gnosis* is "knowledge," and acquiring

PISTIS:
belief, faith

PISTOS:
faithful

knowledge requires mental activity; *elpis* is "hope," and obtaining hope requires mental activity; and *apokalupsis* is revelation—the revealing of something, again, an act that requires mental activity. One must assume, then, that an action of our minds is essential to having "faith," *pistis.*

It is of more than passing interest that the book of

Hebrews contains a complete chapter listing Old Testament heroes who exemplified faith (chapter 11). Paul presents these heroes as people who did great deeds; but he insists in each instance that they were able to perform their great deeds *because of faith*. While Paul noted their achievements to stimulate us to accomplish great things for God, too, these records also imply that whoever wishes to achieve wonderful things for God must do so *by means of faith*. Again, this suggests that we must believe, first, that God really exists, and, second, that He rewards those who trust Him.

If we wish to serve the Lord, especially in these last days of the world's history, we must have faith—which calls to mind the sad observation Jesus made when He concluded His parable of the "Dangerous Widow" (see chapter 7 of this book). In that parable, He illustrated how very willing His heavenly Father was (and is) to help us in our difficult situations. "Nevertheless," Jesus said, "when the Son of man has come, He won't find faith upon the earth, will He?" (Luke 18:8; author's translation).

Jesus' comment is a warning that in the last days, faith will be almost nonexistent—perhaps even among those who claim to be following Him. The lesson here should be clear: we who are living in the last days must school ourselves diligently to have faith in God—to trust Him always, even when we can't see clearly the path ahead of us. Then, when the final upheavals of earthly history take place, we at least will be among those "faith-full" ones through whom God can finish His work for our world.

CHAPTER 25

Sprinkle, Pour, or Dunk?

Sometimes when theologians discuss the Christian ritual of baptism, they give the impression that we can learn all we need to know about how it should be done by studying the practice of the church down through the ages. It seems, though, that we should give more weight to the meaning of the name of this ancient rite. When we know what *baptism* means, we'll have a firmer concept of how the rite should be performed. Unfortunately, too often people have ignored this approach, which has resulted in numerous Christian organizations substituting some rather weak forms of baptism—such as "pouring" and even "sprinkling"—in place of that which the Bible calls for.

The English word *baptism* itself is derived from the Greek noun *baptisma*. This noun itself was derived from the Greek verb *baptizō*, which, in turn, was derived from the more ancient Greek verb *baptō*. This last verb signified the act of *thrusting into or under a liquid*. Originally, it denoted something like "to immerse" or even "to dunk," and in its later usage it came to mean simply *to completely cover (with a liquid)*. *Baptō* occurs three times in the Greek Bible, in each case with this meaning. Matthew 26:23 and Mark 14:20 picture the thrusting of the tip of one's finger into a liquid, and in Revelation 19:13, John describes the garments of the Son of God as having been dipped in blood.

The Greek verb *baptizō* was used more frequently in the New Testament than *baptō* was. It was developed by inserting the syllable *–iz–* into *baptō*. That gave the word a causative nuance—"to cause to be immersed." Then, to fill the need for a noun, the suffix *–ma* was added to the verb *baptizō*, forming the word *baptisma*. In ancient Greek, the suffix *–ma* indicated that the noun represented the result of an activity, so *baptisma* means something like "the result of being immersed," or "the result of having been immersed."

In Greek writings before New Testament times, the verbal forms were used to depict the action of totally immersing people or objects in a liquid—typically, in water. The words could be used in a figurative sense: an ancient Attic author, for instance, wrote of a man whom he said was "baptized in debt"—an expression similar to our "drowning in debt." Certainly, this expression suggests that poor man was *immersed* in his troubles, not just "sprinkled" by them. Another Greek man who was apparently highly irritated with someone wrote that he wished that person would go out and "baptize himself" in the ocean—which no doubt we can interpret as an "invitation" for the offending party to drown himself! Again, the picture is that of someone being immersed—or in this case, immersing himself—in something.

BAPTIZŌ:

to cause to

be immersed

Thus, in New Testament times, *baptō, baptizō,* and *baptisma* all referred to the act of immersion. They don't imply water being used in any way other than to immerse someone or something. In fact, people who lived in those days would have been surprised and probably even confused if they'd been told that some religionists now speak of an "immersion (*baptism*) by sprinkling" because *baptizō* means placing a person or an object under the surface of water or some other liquid. Therefore, they would consider the idea of immersion by sprinkling to be an oxymoron—a confusion of words that results in meaninglessness. In addition, the biblical metaphors related to baptism—*cleansing* and *burial,* the latter picturing the death of the individual to the old way of life—both involve a total experience, total covering.

CHAPTER 26

Predestined to Eternal Death?

Does God determine ahead of time just who will be saved and who will be lost? According to some people, the answer is Yes. In all honesty, they believe that God decides the destiny of each of us in detail long before we're born— which suggests that we don't have to be concerned about what we do, whether good or bad, because we can't change our destiny. This is called "predestination"—the belief that God predetermined long ago everything that we do and all the results of our actions.

Christians who hold this doctrine claim that it is based on texts found in the New Testament—for instance, texts such as the following, which say that God the Father has "predestinated us unto the adoption of children by Jesus Christ to himself, according to the good pleasure of his will" (Ephesians 1:5, KJV). "We have obtained an inheritance, being predestinated according to the purpose of him who worketh all things after the counsel of his own will" (verse 11, KJV).

What does the New Testament word that is translated "to predestinate" really mean?

The Greek verb that is translated "to predestinate" is *proorizō,* a compound word formed by adding the Greek preposition *pro* to the verb *horizō.* In order to understand the meaning of the compound word, we'll look at the two elements separately and in more detail.

The Greek verb *horizō*—"to determine," "to set," "to limit," etc.—conveys the basic idea of setting a boundary, of establishing limits or limitations. In this connection, it may be helpful to observe that English speakers have created a few

PROORIZŌ:

to set limits

beforehand

words based on the Greek root *horiz–.* For example, our word *horizon,* a term that refers to the limits of our sight, is based on that Greek root. Another word based on that root was placed on signs that marked the boundaries of heathen temples. Those signs were erected to mark the limits of the temple property and to warn people not to move carelessly onto sacred ground.

The same verb appears in Acts 17:26. Paul used it of the boundaries God established around various nations and the temporal limitations of their existence. As the King James Version put it, God "*hath determined* the times before appointed, and the bounds of their habitation" (emphasis added). It should be of more than passing interest to observe that in this particular context, Paul immediately pointed out the purpose of this divine act: "that they should seek the Lord" (verse 27, KJV). So God didn't set those limits in order to predestinate anyone either to gain or to lose salvation. Rather, He did so to make it easier for people to seek and to find Him.

The preposition *pro* was frequently employed as a prefix

in compound words such as *proorizō* to indicate that the activity specified by the main verbal root was accomplished beforehand. So, read quite simply and literally, the compound verb *proorizō* means "to set limits beforehand."

It would appear, then, that wherever the verb *proorizō* appears in the New Testament, where it is typically rendered "to predestinate" or something similar, the point was certainly not that God was excluding people from salvation *before* they chose one way or another, nor that He was guaranteeing anyone salvation in advance. Rather, the expression simply means that God has set up various boundaries and limitations on individuals as well as upon nations, and we may read His intention in this: He has done so with their salvation in mind.

All human beings face limits of many kinds. They can see only so far with their unaided eyes. Their ears can hear only those sounds that fall between certain limits. No matter how hard they train, they can run only so fast, and lift only so much weight. There are even definite limitations on how long they can live. Sometimes, with practice and with the aid of various devices, human beings can push somewhat beyond the normal limits. But then they meet new limits that say, "No farther!"

We must remember that God has established the limits that restrain us in order to benefit us. As the verb in Acts 17:26, 27 implies in its fuller context, He has provided these boundaries as aids to help us in our search for Him, never as barriers to keep us from Him.

Scripture points out that we run into limits even in our search to understand the things of God. Zophar asked Job, "Can you find out the deep things of God? Can you find out the limit of the Almighty?" (Job 11:7). There will be times when we can't comprehend everything we would like to know about God. As we are informed in Deuteronomy 29:29, "The secret things belong unto the Lord our God" (KJV).

So, obviously, there are things in life that we cannot hope to understand. There are limits to our learning. However, Moses concludes in this verse in Deuteronomy that even though we must admit these limitations, "the revealed things belong to us and to our children forever, to observe all the words of this law."

CHAPTER 27

Can a Soul Die?

A large majority of Christians believe that human souls can't die, but several biblical passages indicate that the soul is mortal. So the question that comprises the title of this chapter is certainly a legitimate one, and because it involves such an important matter—or at least one that we tend to think is important!—we might even say the question is a vital one.

To get at the heart of this question and to understand the New Testament passages that impinge on it, we must first take a brief look at the Old Testament concept of a soul. We'll start at the very beginning: with the Bible's record of the creation of human beings.

The Bible gives no indication that human souls existed prior to the creation of the first man and woman. The writer of the book of Genesis gives a precise description of the beginning of the race: "The LORD God formed man of the dust of the ground, and breathed into his nostrils the breath of life; and man *became a living soul*" (Genesis 2:7, KJV; emphasis added). This description—so simple, direct, and clear—doesn't say that the first human being *obtained* a living soul when he was created, but that he "*became* a living soul."

This description of how humankind was created strongly implies that the English word *soul* is a translation of a term that in the Hebrew Bible designated a *complete human being*. In fact, modern English versions of the Bible translate the last few words of Genesis 2:7 in that very way, quite correctly saying that "man became a living *being*"—again revealing the broad meaning of this word.

The Old Testament Hebrew word that most often stands behind the word *soul* in our English Bibles is *nephesh*. This word can be found in the other Semitic languages of the Near East—and in nearly all of these languages, it means the *complete person*. A person doesn't *possess* a *nephesh*, he or she *is* a *nephesh*. And the Hebrew specifically says that a *nephesh* can die. In fact, the Old Testament states that death is the penalty for *every* soul that sins—Ezekiel 18:4 makes the unambiguous declaration, "The soul [*nephesh*] that sinneth, it shall die" (KJV).

The New Testament Greek word more or less equivalent to the Hebrew *nephesh* is *psuchē*, a word that also often means the entire person. For instance, in Acts 2:41 the early church is described as growing by the addition of "about three thousand souls" (KJV). Similarly, in Acts 27:37, *psuchē* is used in a statement about the number of passengers who were on board the ship upon which Paul was traveling: "We were in all in the ship, two hundred threescore and sixteen souls" (KJV). And John used *psuchē* when he was describing the effects of an end-time punishment: "The second angel poured out his vial upon the sea; and it became as the blood of a dead man: and every living soul [*psuchē*] died in the sea" (Revelation 16:3, KJV).

Significantly, he may have been using *psuchē* of animals as well as of human beings.

In other passages, however, the Greek term seems to refer particularly to the human mind in its role as the seat of thought, emotions, and reactions. Thus, it occurs in the context of Christ's anticipating His crucifixion. He is described as saying, "Now is my *soul* troubled" (John 12:27, KJV; emphasis added), and when He was praying in the Garden of Gethsemane, He said, "My *soul* is exceeding sorrowful, even unto death" (Matthew 26:38, KJV; emphasis added). In other New Testament passages, *psuchē* means people's character or even their religious experience—their standing before God as recorded in heaven's books. For example, Christ posed the thought-provoking question: "What is a man profited, if he shall gain the whole world, and lose his own *soul*? or what shall a man give in exchange for his *soul*?" (Matthew 16:26, KJV; emphasis added).

NEPHESH: *soul; being*

PSUCHĒ: *soul; person; mind; character; life*

Thus, the Greek term *psuchē* seems to have had a broader meaning than the Hebrew term *nephesh* did. While *nephesh* sometimes designated the mind or even the personality as representative of the whole person, *psuchē* was used more frequently in these senses. In Matthew 22:37, for instance, Christ refers to our need to love God "with all thy heart [i.e., with all of one's emotional powers], and with all thy *soul* [i.e., with all of one's *thinking powers*], and with all thy mind [with all of one's wisdom]" (KJV; emphasis added).

Psuchē easily shaded into the concepts that were basic to *nephesh,* so in many contexts in the New Testament, the word *soul* may mean a person's life as a complete and independent entity. This "soul," then—this "life"—can be judged and ended forever if it doesn't measure up. Christ once told a parable in which He revealed the thoughts of a certain rich man: "I will say to my soul, Soul, thou hast much goods laid up for many years; take thine ease, eat, drink, and be merry. But God said unto him, Thou fool, this night thy soul shall be required of thee: then whose shall those things be, which thou hast provided?" (Luke 12:19, 20, KJV).

Determining the meaning in Scripture of the English word *soul* may at times seem a bit challenging. However, we can usually figure out what it means if we remember that it usually is a rendering of the Hebrew word *nephesh,* the general meaning of which is the human being as a complete entity. The New Testament term often adds to this picture an emphasis upon the emotional, mental, and spiritual aspects of the individual human being.

CHAPTER 28

Spooky Spirits—or Just the Wind?

If asked whether or not we human beings have a spirit, most Christians are likely to say Yes. What they mean by that is complicated by two beliefs that many people consider fundamental to Christianity even though there's little or no biblical support for them.

The two complicating beliefs are, first, that the biblical terms translated "soul" (Hebrew, *nephesh,* and Greek, *psuchē*) and "spirit" (Hebrew, *ruach,* and Greek, *pneuma*) are essentially synonyms, referring to a single entity; and second, that at death this entity leaves our bodies and thereafter lives eternally either in God's presence in a place called heaven or in a place of punishment called hell.

In contrast, I believe, first, that the two biblical terms depict two different entities, and second, that the Bible doesn't use either term to depict the after-death experience, although these terms may sometimes appear in the Bible's descriptions of events related to death. Instead, the Bible uses both words to describe particular aspects of our earthy, bodily makeup. So, we need to examine these terms in some detail in order to determine just what the writers of

Scripture intended when they used these words.

Any serious study of the words *soul* and *spirit* should probably begin with a careful look at Genesis 2:7. This passage of Scripture draws the curtain back on the creation of the first human being. It provides us, in rather simple and easy-to-understand language, a helpful summary of what went into the creation of the human race: "The LORD God formed man from the dust of the ground, and breathed into his nostrils the breath of life; and the man became a living being."

This passage informs us that the Creator initially gathered a number of chemical and mineral elements from the ground and molded them into the body of the man—a body that was, however, not yet a living entity. Next,

RUACH; PNEUMA:

wind; spirit; Spirit

God breathed into the nostrils of this body, and the body became a *nephesh*—a soul, a "living being." No doubt we can justifiably assume that on that occasion the Deity's act of breathing was far different from any breathing that a human being can do, because no person yet has formed a creature of clay and then made it live just by blowing air into its nostrils. God's animating breath must have contained some power unknown to us. But to return to our discussion, note the formula: God's breath plus the lifeless body yields a *nephesh*, a living soul, a living being.

God's animating breath was a life-giving or life-producing movement of air, which, in human terms, is wind. In Hebrew, it's the word *ruach* that means wind. The context of passages such as Exodus 10:13, "The LORD brought an east wind upon the land," and Exodus 14:21, "The LORD drove the sea back by a strong east wind," reveals that the Hebrew term means, simply, a literal wind—air in motion. However, in certain Old Testament contexts, it appears that the term *ruach,* often translated "spirit" in these contexts, was used of an energizing or electrifying forcefulness that drives our thinking and pushes us to achieve some goal—an aggressive mood that enables us to accomplish something. The lessening or intermittent functioning of this force in one's thinking may produce a state of depression, and, conversely, its renewal may revitalize a person's energies. Jacob, for instance, sank into depression over his loss of Joseph; but when he discovered that Joseph was still alive, "the spirit of their father Jacob revived" (Genesis 45:27). When this electrifying force completely stops functioning in the human brain, the person dies.

This same term, *ruach,* was used to designate the Third Member of the Godhead. In those cases, English translations typically render it as "Spirit." For instance, in Genesis 1:2, this mighty Person is presented in the words, "the Spirit of God was hovering over the face of the waters" (NKJV).

The New Testament Greek word that corresponds to *ruach* is *pneuma,* a word that, like *ruach,* basically means "air in motion," or "wind." In the majority of the New Testament passages in which *pneuma* appears, the reference is to the invisible forces that surround us. In some of these passages, for instance, the word *spirit* is accompanied by the word *unclean,* and the usage obviously refers to fallen or apostate angels. (See, e.g., Matthew 10:1; 12:43; Mark 1:23, 26, 27; 3:11; etc.) At times, though, *pneuma* refers to the commanding or driving force of a person's own will—a force that compels people to act on the ideas their minds

Page 122

have devised. Thus in many New Testament contexts, the word *pneuma* seems to represent mental activity, the varied actions of the brain. Such mental activity seems to be the major significance of *pneuma* in Matthew 26:41; Mark 2:8; 8:12; Luke 1:47, 80; 2:40; 23:46; etc.

And, as is true of *ruach, pneuma* also refers to the Third Member of the Godhead. In this usage, *pneuma* is often modified by the adjective "Holy" (as in Luke 11:13) or by some qualifying phrase such as the expression the "Spirit of God" (see Matthew 3:16) and the "Spirit of the Lord" (see Luke 4:18). Many times, however, the Holy Spirit is referred to in the New Testament simply as the *Spirit* (e.g., Acts 2:4, 17, 18, etc.). Interestingly, in John 3:8, *pneuma* means both "wind" and "spirit": "The wind blows where it chooses, and you hear the sound of it, but you do not know where it comes from or where it goes. So it is with everyone who is born of the Spirit." *Pneuma* appears twice in this verse; in the first case it is translated "wind," and in the second, "Spirit."

This cursory examination of the usage of the concepts of "soul" and "spirit" reveals a biblical usage that expects or even demands that the two concepts be separated. The word "soul" represents the whole personhood of a sentient human being, while in most cases the word "spirit" designates the decision-making powers of human beings, though in the Genesis account of humankind's creation, *ruach* refers to the unique invigorating power—the divine "breath"—that vitalized the newly created man and made him into a living being. In this specialized use of *breath,* we are, of course, dealing with the powers of Deity— unknowable, though we witness its effects in the continuance of our daily life, which otherwise would cease.

The whole process started with the creation of Adam. This first man was formed from the elements of the earth and became a "living soul" when he received the infilling breath of God. At death, the sequence is reversed: without the all-important breath of God, people become in effect "dead souls."

Do we possess a *spirit?* Yes. As long as God's vitalizing breath maintains our living state and our brain is alive, we can think and live and act; thus our *spirit* electrifies our systems, driving our minds and bodies to live and to carry out what we have willed—ideally, under God's guidance. Thus, we demonstrate that we *do* have a spirit and all is well!

CHAPTER 29

Death: Shortcut to Heaven?

When believers die, do their souls go to dwell with the Lord? Many scholars have voiced their opinion that, Yes, that's what Philippians 1:23 tells us. The matter is of more than passing interest and has occasionally been the subject of heated theological debates. For instance, approximately a half century ago, the esteemed theologian Walter Martin presented a number of arguments in support of this interpretation of the passage.[1]

In the King James Version, Philippians 1:23, 24, reads thus: "I am in a strait betwixt two, having a desire to depart, and to be with Christ; which is far better: Nevertheless to abide in the flesh is more needful for you." This rendering does seem to offer some basis for the position promoted by Dr. Martin and others. But we may well ask whether the Greek manuscripts give any better insight into the meaning of this passage. Do they give grounds for seeing some other meaning in what Paul wrote than that suggested by theologians such as Dr. Martin?

---

1. See Walter R. Martin, *The Truth About Seventh-day Adventism* (Grand Rapids, Mich.: Zondervan, 1960), 122ff; see especially 124f.

Actually, the wording of these verses in the Greek manuscripts most certainly does not support the interpretation
Dr. Martin has proposed. In fact, the passage in the Greek
original so obviously and categorically differs from the position he and others have taken that it is surprising so few
have noticed and written about the real meaning of these
lines.

A verse or two before those with which we are concerned, the apostle, who is imprisoned at the time, mentions two options: he can continue to live, or he can die
(see Philippians 1:20, 21). The first possibility might well
have seemed less attractive for the apostle than we might
assume because it meant he would have to endure a lot of
suffering. In another epistle he writes about just what it
meant to be a missionary of the infant Christian church.
Speaking of others who claimed to be Christians but who
were challenging his authority and calling, he says,

> Are they ministers of Christ? I am talking like a
> madman—I am a better one: with far greater labors,
> far more imprisonments, with countless floggings,
> and often near death. Five times I have received
> from the Jews the forty lashes minus one. Three
> times I was beaten with rods. Once I received a ston-
> ing. Three times I was shipwrecked; for a night and
> a day I was adrift at sea; on frequent journeys, in
> danger from rivers, danger from bandits, danger
> from my own people, danger from Gentiles, danger
> in the city, danger in the wilderness, danger at sea,
> danger from false brothers and sisters; in toil and
> hardship, through many a sleepless night, hungry
> and thirsty, often without food, cold and naked.

And, besides other things, I am under daily pressure because of my anxiety for all the churches (2 Corinthians 11:23–28).

In the light of Paul's experience, one might not have blamed him if he occasionally wondered whether it wouldn't be easier to rest in the grave than to go on exposing himself to continual physical and mental suffering.

But the alternative—namely, to die—couldn't have been an easy choice for him to make either. He felt he had been divinely called to the great missionary campaign he was conducting—traveling across the lands north of the Mediterranean Sea, raising up congregations of believers everywhere he went, and encouraging the new converts. If he were to die, who would take his place? He felt responsible. He felt compelled to carry on no matter what the consequences might be to himself.

In Philippians 1:20, he makes it clear that whatever choice he (or the Lord) should make, he wants the result to be such that "Christ will be exalted now as always in my body, whether by life or by death." In the next verse he then briefly adds that either choice can result only in good: to go on living "is Christ"—presumably, meaning that Christ's cause will be advanced if Paul continues his life—"and dying is gain," which suggests that he personally would "gain" in that his sufferings would end.

In the first part of verse 22, Paul returns to the results of his continuing to live—he would have the satisfaction of "fruitful labor." It is in the rendering of the last sentence of this verse that the King James Version and most modern translations begin to lose Paul's thought. The King James translators rendered the sentence as "yet what I shall choose

I wot not." *Wot* is an old English verb that means "know," so "I wot not" means "I don't know." In other words, this translation says that Paul could choose between dying and continuing to live, but that he didn't know which he would choose.

However, the context suggests Paul really *did* know which choice he was making. It's quite important that we understand the Greek verb Paul used in this verse. The critical word is *gnōrizō,* a verb derived from the verb *ginōskō,* "to know." But *gnōrizō* contains the causative syllable *iz,* which makes the primary meaning of the resultant verbal form not "I know," but "I cause to know," or, in other words, "I inform." In the clause we're examining, Paul also used a negative, the equivalent of "not." So, what he actually said wasn't "I don't know," but rather "I'm not informing [you]," "I'm not going to say." And what is it that the apostle won't reveal? *Ti hairēsomai*—"what I shall choose for myself."

This sentence, then, clearly says that *Paul won't disclose whether he will choose to go on living or to die.* The point is that translating the passage in such a way as to have Paul saying that he wishes to die makes him contradict himself, because in this verse he has categorically stated that he won't inform his readers which choice he is making.

GNŌRIZŌ:

I cause to know;

I inform

Paul continues wrestling with the two choices in verse 23 while still keeping his decision to himself. He says, "I am constrained *out* of those two" (author's translation; emphasis added)—in other words, "If it is all the same to you—or to God—I would just as soon not have anything to do with either of those choices." His reaction is utterly understandable. Neither choice is attractive. To go on living is to continue suffering; but dying doesn't sound good either. In fact, Paul says he is "restrained," or "constrained," "away from"—the Greek wording here has the preposition *ek,* which literally means "out of"—these two alternatives.

What would he rather do? Again, we must remember that what we consider Paul's next words to be must not contradict his statement that he won't divulge to his readers which of the two alternatives he will choose. This opens us to the realization that in what follows, Paul is introducing a third alternative. Because he is pulled away from the two possibilities he doesn't want, what can he propose instead?

In the rest of the verse, Paul uses a participle as a *"causal clause equivalent"*—a participle that takes the place of a regular clause and gives a reason for a preceding statement. So, this last part of the sentence means "because I want to leave and be with Christ, for that would be better by far." This translation has the advantage of being much closer to the intent of the entire passage and avoids making Paul contradict himself.

So, Paul concludes his thought by indicating that he doesn't yearn for either of the alternatives—in fact, he is repelled by both of them—and without making a choice between living and dying—or at least without informing anyone about what he's chosen. He then expresses his desire for a third alternative: to depart and be with Christ.

It seems likely, then, that what Paul really wanted was something like what Elijah experienced. That prophet of old didn't have to pass through the grave but rather was transported directly to heaven. Such an end to Paul's life on earth would stop the pains that were his daily as a world-traveling missionary while also avoiding the pangs of death. That, Paul said in effect, "is better by far" than continuing to live and better also than dying.

So, what Paul wanted most was to be transported to heaven immediately without seeing death. He would thereby have avoided the long wait until the day of the final resurrection, when everyone will finally see the Lord (John 11:23, 24; Ecclesiastes 9:5, 6, 10; Matthew 24:31). Unfortunately, he didn't get that third option. He lived a few years longer, still witnessing for his Lord, and then died a martyr's death in Rome.

Was that extended life and witness what Paul chose? We still don't know.

CHAPTER 30

What's the Point of Preaching
to Spirits?

It seems safe to say that 1 Peter 3:19, 20 is one of the most difficult passages in Scripture to explain. It says that by the Spirit, Christ "went and preached to the spirits in prison, who formerly did not obey, when God's patience waited in the days of Noah, during the building of the ark, in which a few, that is, eight persons, were saved through water" (RSV).

Even after the most careful study, one may still be left wondering just what Peter might have meant by these two verses. The widely esteemed theologian Bo Reicke once referred to verse 19 as a "widely disputed remark,"[1] and we don't have to spend many moments reflecting on that verse to realize why he said that.

People of various persuasions have differing attitudes toward these verses. Those theologians who believe that lost sinners and/or lost angels will be given a second opportunity to accept salvation and those who believe in the existence of some sort of purgatory in which sinful beings

---

1. Bo Reicke, *The Epistles of James, Peter, and Jude,* The Anchor Bible (Garden City, N.Y.: Doubleday & Co., 1964), 37:109.

131

can be purged of their sins are happy to take this passage at it's apparent face value. As far as they are concerned, it poses no problem. On the other hand, those who would like to grow in their understanding of Christ's work for the salvation of lost sinners find reason for perplexity as they try to unravel the several threads of thought that run through this somewhat convoluted passage of Scripture. And those who delight in solving puzzles comprised of ancient Greek writing experience surges of joy as they wrestle with some of the apostle's most arcane and intertwined statements.

As we work at understanding this passage, we'll find it useful to begin by determining what theological beliefs we *should not* consider to be possibilities. We must assume that Peter wouldn't have proposed theological positions that contradict other portions of the sacred writings. That means our interpretation must take into account the following three points.

First, while the Bible contains numerous references to prisons and prisoners, for the most part, such passages deal with actual prisons and live prisoners. Few if any of them use these terms as metaphors of death and the deceased. One well-known prophecy does describe the coming Messiah as One who would open prisons for those who are bound, but most theologians think of this prophecy as predicting the release of those who are bound by sin rather than the resurrection of those who are dead.

Second, the Bible doesn't picture dead people as sentient beings.[2] Consequently, it's not likely that the "spirits"

---

2. What was supposedly the departed prophet Samuel in the episode reported in 1 Samuel 28 doubtless was instead an evil angel who was interested only in Saul's ruin.

in 1 Peter 3:19, 20 are dead people who continue to exist in some kind of "spiritual" form. Furthermore, Psalm 146:4, which declares that when a person dies, "his breath goeth forth, he returneth to his earth; *in that very day his thoughts perish*" (KJV; emphasis added. Cf. also Ecclesiastes 9:5).

Third, the Bible is quite consistent in saying that people have only one life to live during the present age and one choice about their eternal welfare to be made during this life. Nowhere else does the Bible hint at anyone's having another chance to make that choice.

In view of these three points, the usual, fanciful interpretations of 1 Peter 3:19, 20 that suggest Christ was off somewhere preaching while His body lay in the tomb[3] lack biblical support. On top of that, they ignore what the grammar and syntax of the Greek text behind this passage suggest.

What is this passage really saying? What does the ancient Greek rendition of the passage tell us about it? A rather literal translation of the two verses should make the point clearer: Christ was made alive by the Spirit, "by means of which

Christ "went and preached to the spirits in prison."

Spirit, when He went [there], He preached to the souls[4] who were in prison, who *were at that time disobedient*—when the patience of God waited for them during the days when Noah was building the ark" (emphasis added).

In translation, the text may be quite cumbersome, but in Greek it seems rather nicely developed. Whatever the case of its literary merit, however, it simply says that the

---

3. See, e.g., Reicke's comments in *James, Peter, and Jude*, 110f.
4. I.e., persons; see, e.g., Ezekiel 18:20 and chapter 18.

Christ who did extensive evangelistic work when He lived on earth also spoke to the hearts of men and women by means of the Holy Spirit during other periods of history. He was just as interested in saving human beings during those times as He was when He was living here as a man. Presumably, His patience is as great now as it was during the time of Noah, and, fortunately for us, He still is actively trying to rescue all of us from the prison of sin.

CHAPTER 31

Is Baptism for the Dead Biblical?

First Corinthians 15:29 is a rather strange text—strange because it seems to speak approvingly of the practice of being baptized for people who have died.

In the King James Version, this verse is rendered: "Else what shall they do which are baptized for the dead, if the dead rise not at all? why are they then baptized for the dead?" The passage is significant because some churches teach that even *after* our friends and relatives have died, we can do something about their ultimate fate by being baptized for them. In fact, some teach that we can even be baptized for our unbelieving ancestors of long ago and thus obtain their salvation. The verse we're concerned with here appears to give those who hold this belief some justification for it. Can we pass on to other people—even dead people—spiritual merit that we've earned? If not, what did Paul mean by this verse?

In the first place, we need to remember that elsewhere, Scripture consistently and clearly says that God will judge each person individually, and He will do so without taking into account the deeds of some other person. For example,

Ezekiel wrote, "Though Noah, Daniel, and Job, were in it [a land, a country], as I live, saith the Lord GOD, they shall deliver neither son nor daughter; they shall but deliver their own souls by their righteousness" (Ezekiel 14:20, KJV; see also verse 14). And the book of Revelation pictures God as saying, "I will give to each of you as your works deserve" (Revelation 2:23).

In addition, the verse we're considering can legitimately be translated and punctuated to read differently from the way it does in the King James Version. It can read instead: "Otherwise, what are those people who are being baptized doing? Are they being baptized for the sake of those who are dead? If dead people are not raised at all, why are people being baptized? Is it for them?" In other words, if people who die are dead forever, what would be the point of baptizing them or being baptized for them? In context, the point seems to be that whether or not being baptized for the dead actually saves them, the fact that people are carrying out this rite shows that they believe in a resurrection.

"Why are they then baptized for the dead?"

This translation takes into account the purpose of the entire context surrounding the verse in question. In the context, which is lengthy, Paul lays down a solid foundation on which the Christian hope of a resurrection to come can stand firm. He begins the chapter with an impressive account of the factuality of Christ's resurrection as noted by a large body of witnesses (1 Corinthians 15:1–11). According to the apostle, Christ's return to life after His crucifixion should be enough to justify our faith, verify the reason for our hope, and encourage us to look forward to the time when through our Savior's power, we also will come forth from the tomb and experience life again, just as He did (verses 12–28). In the rest of the chapter, Paul presents a number of other arguments that buttress the doctrine of the resurrection of believers.

Paul seems to have been throwing into 1 Corinthians 15 every argument for the resurrection that he could think of, including the one in verse 29, which we might think rather strange and which he poses without explanation, almost as an afterthought. There are some people who practice immersion on behalf of dead people, he says. They wouldn't be doing that if they didn't believe there was a resurrection. Paul neither approves nor explains this practice; he merely mentions it as an example of some people in his day who believe in a resurrection, and then he moves on to other evidences of the certainty of this teaching.

The position of the Christian is clear. We believe—and a large and trustworthy group of witnesses confirm—that Christ experienced the resurrection Himself and therefore has obtained on our behalf the keys to death and the grave (Revelation 1:18). According to Paul, this should give us comfort, courage, and especially *hope* for our future. And regardless of how people may interpret 1 Corinthians 15:29, Scripture doesn't support the idea that anyone can rest his or her hope upon merit accumulated by some other human being. Instead, it says our hope of eternal life rests solely upon the acts and grace of both Jesus Christ and the Father and upon our faith in Their provision for our salvation. No one, then, is justified in saying that here, Paul endorsed either the practice of being baptized for the dead or the idea that the dead live on in some intermediate state before the resurrection at Christ's return.

CHAPTER 32

Revelation *About* Jesus or

From Him?

What is the purpose of the book of Revelation? Some interpreters of the Bible say that the first five words[1] of the book, "The revelation of Jesus Christ," answer that question.

These words comprise a phrase made up of an action noun followed by a noun in the genitive (possessive) case. Often when genitive nouns are paired with action nouns, the genitive nouns are the *objects* of the action nouns, telling us what is being acted upon. For example, when someone speaks of the "education of children" or the "catching of fish," we readily understand that the children and the fish are the direct objects of the actions portrayed by the action nouns. These genitive nouns are called *objective genitives*.

Revelation's purpose:

to show us "what

must soon take place."

The first five words of the book of Revelation comprise just such a phrase: the word *revelation* is an action noun

---

1. Five words in English; three in the original Greek.

that names the act of revealing something, and it is followed by a double proper noun in the genitive case—"Jesus Christ." Consequently, some people have concluded that "Jesus Christ" is the *object* of the action noun "revelation." In other words, they claim that the apostle John meant this phrase to say that the purpose of the book of Revelation is to reveal Jesus Christ.

However, phrases such as "the bark of the dog" and "the cry of the baby" warn us that genitive nouns aren't always the object of action nouns. No, in cases such as these latter two examples, the nouns in the genitive case identify who or what is acting, who or what is doing the action. So, for example, the baby isn't the *object* of the crying; it's the baby that is acting, that is *doing* the crying. Nouns in the genitive case that identify who or what is doing the action are called *subjective genitives.* If the words "Jesus Christ" in the first line of Revelation 1 were subjective genitives, that line wouldn't mean that Jesus was the object of the revealing, the One being revealed; rather, it would mean that Jesus is the One who is doing the revealing.

How can we tell whether a noun in the genitive case linked to an action noun is to be interpreted as the subject of the action noun or its object—whether the genitive noun is doing the action or receiving the action?

The immediate context is of prime importance here. We must carefully consider the line of thought preceding and following the two nouns and find an interpretation that harmonizes with the context.

In the case we've been focusing on, a careful reading of the context tells us that Revelation 1:1 isn't picturing Jesus Christ as the object of the revelation. The first words after the opening phrase inform us that "God gave him" this revelation. Why would God give to Jesus Christ a revelation about Jesus Christ? The context, then, indicates that it isn't logical to say that Jesus Christ is the object of the revelation. Rather, the phrase "of Jesus Christ" is an ordinary genitive with a possessive force. It means that God gave a revelation to Jesus Christ that Jesus then "possessed." Furthermore, the context continues—specifically stating in the very next words the actual purpose of the book of Revelation: "to show his servants what must soon take place."[2] And the rest of the verse completes the picture. In it, John tells how he got the prophecy that the book contains: God gave the revelation to Jesus Christ, who "made it known by sending his angel to his servant John."

Of course, the purpose of all the Scripture is to reveal the activities of the Godhead in Their work of redeeming everyone possible. So we could certainly say that the purpose of the book of Revelation is to reveal Christ—and to reveal God the Father and to reveal the Holy Spirit. But that's not what John was writing about in Revelation 1:1. No, in this verse he categorically says the primary purpose of the book of Revelation is something different. It's to show God's servants a preview of future events.

---

2. A purposive infinitive, "to show," begins the line stating the purpose of the book—further indication that this interpretation is correct.

CHAPTER 33

The Days of Rage and Danger

According to one of the ancient Athenian historians, Clearchus was one of the most successful of all Greek military commanders. He knew how to lead large groups of soldiers into battle in such a way that they always were victorious. Of course, the common soldiers loved having him plan the strategy.

But Clearchus had one distinct weakness—a weakness that gave many a soldier of that time second thoughts about joining this general's army. Although Clearchus was a brilliant military strategist, he had a terribly violent temper. In camp, he was a terror. It didn't take much to send him into a fit of rage; and when he was angry, he was frighteningly dangerous. People who happened to be anywhere near the general when he lost his temper about something could lose their lives.

What has Clearchus to do with Bible study? The older English versions translate a phrase Paul wrote describing the end times as "perilous times" (2 Timothy 3:1, KJV). But the Greek wording Paul used seems to imply somewhat more than is contained in the simple phrase "perilous times." He actually wrote that in the very last days of this world, "there will be *chalepoi* times." That Greek word is the same adjective as was used to describe the outbursts of anger that were so alarmingly dangerous to those around Clearchus.

CHALEPOS:

hard; violent; dangerous; stressful; evil

In other words, the angry outbursts of that general of old provide us with a window into what we may expect to be an important characteristic of the end times: *chalepoi* times. In the last days, we can expect to see human beings exhibiting *unusual outbursts of anger toward one another*—the kind of anger that *endangers peoples' lives*.

John the revelator also pictured this characteristic of the last days. He wrote,

The nations *raged*,
    but your wrath has come,
    and the time for judging the dead,
for rewarding your servants, the prophets
    and saints and all who fear your name
    both small and great,
and for destroying those who destroy the earth
        (Revelation 11:18; emphasis added).

Today, fanatical religious and political organizations boldly teach their adherents to express their rage even by self-destruction if need be in order to destroy the objects of their anger. When the followers of Christ witness these astonishing manifestations of fanatical, dangerous wrath multiplying in the world today, they recognize them as vivid evidence that we are surely already living in the days that the prophecy of long ago pictured for us. They see in it clear evidence that Jesus' return cannot be far in the future.

CHAPTER 34

Who Is the *Antichrist?*

Through most of the Christian era, the term *antichrist* has appeared frequently in Christian literature. However, during the apostolic age, this label was seldom used, showing up only in the pastoral letters of the apostle John. As a theological concept, *antichrist* has come to be thought of by many people as referring to someone who is or was a special opponent of Christ. It's likely that this idea has been derived from what the prefix *anti* means in English: "against," "opposed to," "contrary to," etc.

It's true that the Greek preposition *anti* sometimes—especially in compound words—was used to express the idea of being opposed to someone or something. See, for instance, such New Testament terms as *antipiptein*, "to resist"; *antidikos*, "an opponent in a lawsuit"; and *antilegein* "to speak against" or "to oppose," etc. But scholars of the Greek language have pointed out that *anti* has other important meanings as well, some of which show up in the New Testament. For instance, in some places, this preposition says its object is located *across the way* from the subject, occasionally indicating that someone is close enough to be able to reach out and help someone else. This seems to be the meaning this preposition contributes to the Greek verb Paul used in the first sentence of Romans 8:26: "The Spirit helps [*sun*anti*lambanetai*] us in our weakness."

However, another highly important and frequently seen usage of this term expresses the concept of something or someone being a *substitute* for something or someone else. Mark 10:45 contains an example of this usage. *Anti* is translated as "for" in the last phrase of the verse—and "for" is obviously used in the sense of "as a substitute for": "The Son of man came not to be served but to serve, and to give his life a ransom *for* many" (emphasis added). We find another example in Matthew 2:22. In explaining why Joseph took Mary and Jesus to Nazareth rather than back to Bethlehem when they returned from Egypt, Matthew wrote, "When he [Joseph] heard that Archelaus was ruling over Judea *in place of* [*anti*] his father Herod, he was afraid to go there" (emphasis added).

Substitution may be one of the most important meanings *anti* has in the New Testament. In fact, the proposition that in the compound word *antichrist, anti* conveys primarily the idea of substitution, may be easier to defend than that it means something like "opposer of." If John meant *antichrist* simply to picture those who have *opposed* Christ, we would never be able to determine whom the label fits because through the millennia since He lived on earth, uncounted millions of people have opposed Him. But a prophetic warning regarding someone who would presume to proclaim himself to be *a*

ANTI:

a substitute for something or someone else

substitute for Christ is full of meaning.

In past centuries, Protestants thought of the bishop of Rome as the embodiment of the New Testament antichrist. Is that a valid application of this term?

It isn't especially difficult to find the answer. We've seen that the term can be defined as something like "substitute for Christ." Significantly, the pope, the head of the Roman Catholic Church, has assumed the title of *Vicarius Filii Dei* ("Vicar of the Son of God"). The primary meaning of both *vicar* and *vicarious* is "substitute." Thus, by insisting that their chief bishop is the vicar of Christ, the Catholic Church is, at the same time, insisting that he is the *antichrist*—a substitute for Christ, someone who takes His place.

CHAPTER 35

The Ultimate Test of Loyalty

The Greek word *kurios* means "lord" or "master." It's the title of someone who has absolute control over one or more other human beings. Those who bore this title had the power to buy and sell other people and even, at times, to decide whether they lived or died—obviously, a master/ slave relationship. In addition, some administrative advisors to the Roman emperors suggested that the term even contained a hint of divinity, and, in fact, for quite some time, the Jews had employed the word as a title of the Great Creator God Himself.

Eventually, however, the emperors of Rome adopted the title *kurios* and began to demand that people use it when they addressed them. Then someone in the administrative circles of the government decided that all the people in the empire should be required to declare in front of a government official that the emperor was their *kurios,* their absolute master, and that they should publicly renounce all other lords. Christians felt extremely uncomfortable about making declarations to that effect since they referred to Jesus Christ as their *kurios.* Thousands of them got into trouble because they refused to make these declarations.

Eventually, the Roman government ruled that a refusal to recognize the emperor as the absolute *kurios* was a capital offense against the government. The historical records of those days indicate that at that time, many Christians—possibly tens or even hundreds of thousands—sealed their faith by dying a martyr's death because of their loyalty to Christ rather than to Caesar as their *kurios*. They chose to become the sport of lions in the Roman amphitheaters or to experience many other sorts of horrific torture in order to continue in their allegiance to the One whom they worshiped as their true Lord.

KURIOS:

lord; master

During the apostolic age, then, stating in public one's conviction that Jesus Christ was Lord was a life-and-death matter. In those days people didn't make such a statement carelessly. The commitment people had to have to make such a statement may be the reason the apostle Paul told the believers in Rome, "If you confess with your lips that Jesus is Lord and believe in your heart that God raised him from the dead, you will be saved" (Romans 10:9).

Would we today be slow to voice our loyalty to Christ if doing so subjected us to the threat of death? What would it take to cause us to view our allegiance to Him as a life-and-death matter? We should give careful thought to these questions because our eternal life actually *does* depend on whether or not we choose to allow Christ to be the Lord of our life—which makes that decision more important than any other that we might be facing. We would be wise to decide before another day goes past to acknowledge Him as our *kurios,* our Lord, for today and forevermore.

CHAPTER 36

Lost Words

It's strange but true that there are a few words in the Greek New Testament whose meanings have been completely lost. The translations suggested for such words have typically been arrived at by shrewd guesswork sometimes based on the context of the word and sometimes on words thought to be related to the "lost" one. We hope the translations of such words are, for the most part, close to the thoughts the writers were originally intended, but who can tell?

Sometimes, a "lost word" and a suggested definition find their way into Greek/English dictionaries. Occasionally this leads people to conclude that the meaning of this word has finally been established. Good dictionaries indicate the standing of these problem words.

Fortunately, most of the New Testament's lost words aren't in passages that have great significance for our salvation. Nevertheless, these expressions are often in interesting passages; and we can only hope that eventually their meanings will be determined.

Raka, a Greek term used in Matthew 5:22, is one of

these lost words. It is teamed up with a word that means "fool" and occurs in a context that condemns acting out in anger toward other people. Hence, it has been assumed that *raka* was a bad name used to insult someone. Apparently, the term was so foul that Christians stopped using it, which, of course, Christ had admonished them to do. Eventually, the term fell completely out of people's vocabularies—so much so that they forgot what it meant. That has left us guessing. In fact, the expression is so completely dead now that scholars aren't even sure whether it was originally an Aramaic or a Greek term. It will doubtless never be resurrected to function as a word again.

The book of Revelation contains a number of Greek words of doubtful meaning. For example, it mentions a garment called a *podērēs* (see Revelation 1:13). In the King James Version, this noun has been rendered as "a garment down to the foot"—a translation that is at best an educated guess. People have assumed, based on the context, that this garment must have been some type of long royal robe. Exactly what it was like, no one knows.

Another Greek word whose meaning we don't know is found in Revelation 1:15 and 2:18. This word, *chalkolibanos,* appears in both verses as the name of a metal or alloy to which Christ's feet are compared. That it may have been an alloy of some type is suggested in that Revelation 1:15 speaks of it being refined in a furnace. The King James Version calls it "fine brass"; and the New Revised Standard Version, "burnished bronze." Its nature is especially puzzling because its name suggests a strange compound of *chalkos*—copper or brass—and *libanos*—incense. This is such an unlikely mixture that the nature of the amalgam remains a mystery.

Revelation 4:3 and 21:11, 18–20 mention a sizeable number of precious stones, the names of which we still use. However, there is no way of determining whether the names used by John the revelator were attached to the same kinds of gems then as they are today. In other words, when we read such names as topaz, chrysolite, and beryl in Revelation, we have no guarantee that the gems John had in mind are the same as the ones we connect to those names.

Probably the lost word that readers of the New Testament would most like to have defined is the adjective *epiousios*. People consider the loss of this word serious because it's in the Lord's Prayer (see Matthew 6:11). We can be pardoned for wondering how such an important term could ever be lost when so many Christians have prayed this prayer over the years.

RAKA: ?

PODĒRĒS: ?

EPIOUSIOS: ?

Apparently, *epiousios* is an adjective that modifies *bread*. Christians have typically regarded it as meaning "daily" or "sufficient for the day" or something similar, but there's nothing about this word that resembles the Greek term for *day*. There seems to be no easy way to determine just what *epiousios* means, so when we pray the Lord's Prayer and ask for our "*epiousios* bread" to be given us, we can't be sure just what we're asking for!

Perhaps the loss of this word is an example of people's using a word so frequently and in such an unthinking way that they just assume everyone understands the word. Then, children who learned the prayer from their parents did so without learning what the sacred words they faithfully memorized meant. In time, this term lost its significance for those who used it—possibly because it wasn't employed as commonly in daily speech as were the other words in the prayer.

It may be that the meaning of most if not all the other lost words of the New Testament disappeared in the same way as did *epiousios.* We can be grateful that the loss of these words hasn't seriously affected what the New Testament writers had to say about salvation.

APPENDIX

Which Version
Should We Use?

In some passages, the old-fashioned language of the King James Version of the Bible seems to be something closer to a foreign language than it does to the form of English that we've heard and spoken since our childhood days. For example, the King James Version rendering of 2 Corinthians 8:1—"Moreover, brethren, we do you to wit of the grace of God bestowed on the churches of Macedonia"—seems quite foreign to our eyes (and ears), and sometimes we're tempted to just skim over such passages and move on to others that are easier to understand.

The King James Version (KJV) was first published in A.D. 1611. Though it's been revised a bit since then, it still reflects the form of English that was spoken in England four hundred years or more ago. The language this version contains is that which well-educated English people from the upper classes used in conversing with one another. It has always had an attractive dignity that has endeared it to many people.

Some people who have read the KJV from childhood

and have come to treasure it seem not to worry about how understandable it is. However, in the past four centuries, the English language has changed dramatically. Even the speech of the well-educated of America and England no longer sounds like that which was used in 1611. In fact, both the grammar and the vocabulary of the language have changed noticeably. So, in order to understand what they're reading, people must choose between becoming familiar with the form of English employed in 1611 on the one hand and, on the other, procuring a translation of the Bible that uses modern English.

Actually, it's not too difficult to learn the main features of seventeenth-century English. A few points, in fact, will go a long way toward increasing understanding: (1) *Thou* means "you," singular, and *ye* means "you," plural. (2) Second-person present-tense verbal forms end with a *–t* or an *–st;* for instance, "thou art" (*you are,* Matthew 22:16), "thou shalt" (*you shall,* Matthew 23:27), and "thou sayest" (*you say,* Matthew 27:11). (3) Third-person singular verbs end with a *–th,* so you'll see expressions such as "Pilate saith" (*Pilate says,* Matthew 27:22), "he that dippeth" (*he dips,* Matthew 26:23); and "the devil taketh" (*the devil takes,* Matthew 4:8).

In seventeenth-century English, the present tense of the verb *to go* is conjugated as follows:

I go	we go
thou goest	ye go
he/she goeth	they go

Similarly, the verb *to be* is conjugated thus:

I am	we are
thou art	ye are
he/she/it is	they are

The pronoun *you* takes the following forms:

> thou/ye (nominative singular/plural—the
> subject[s] of a verb=*you*)
> thy/thine (possessive forms=*your*)
> thee (direct object of a verb=*you*)

There are some distinct differences in vocabulary between the language of the KJV and the language we speak today. Some words common four hundred years ago have since fallen out of use, and others are still used today, but with a different meaning. Thus one may encounter such words as *wroth* ("angry") and *wot* ("know"—see *"I wot not,"* meaning "I do not know," in Philippians 1:23; cf. chapter 29). The line "we do you to wit" in 2 Corinthians 8:1 means "we inform you," but in 2 Corinthians 5:19, "to wit" means "namely." And the term *conversation,* as found in several texts, such as Galatians 1:13 and Ephesians 4:22, doesn't refer to an exchange of words between two or more people. Instead, it means "conduct," or "manner of living." For the most part, good English dictionaries offer help in understanding the meaning of words we don't recognize or that have come to mean something different than they did when the KJV was produced.

On the other hand, rather than attempting to learn the language of the seventeenth century, we can turn to one of the modern versions. In them the Hebrew, Aramaic, and Greek documents that comprise the Bible have been translated into the English of today. These versions vary from the rather literal—such as the New American Standard Bible (NASB), Revised Standard Version (RSV), New Revised Standard Version (NRSV), Holman Study Bible, and the New King James Version (NKJV)—to freer translations, which range all the way from the middle-of-the-road New International Version (NIV) through the New Living Translation (NLT) to paraphrases such as *The Message* and *The Clear Word*. Of course, there are many other versions that I haven't mentioned here that fit somewhere on the continuum from literal to paraphrastic.

We should use the versions that are rather free paraphrases with some caution when we're trying to establish the precise meanings of specific texts. Such versions serve best when we want to do a quick survey of a large portion of Scripture—when we're reading a chapter or more at a time.

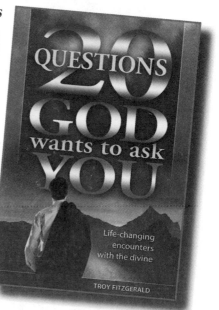